Dicta and Contradicta

Dicta and Contradicta

KARL KRAUS

Translated from the German by Jonathan McVity

UNIVERSITY OF ILLINOIS PRESS   URBANA & CHICAGO

English-language translation © 2001 by the Board of
Trustees of the University of Illinois

Manufactured in the United States of America

∞ This book is printed on acid-free paper.

Library of Congress Cataloging-in-Publication Data
    Kraus, Karl, 1874–1936.
    [Sprüche und Widersprüche. English]
    Dicta and contradicta / Karl Kraus ; translated from the
    German by Jonathan McVity.
      p.   cm.
    Includes bibliographical references and index.
    ISBN 0-252-02648-9 (alk. paper)
    I. Title.
    PT2621.R27S613   2001
    838'.91202—dc21   00-011155

C 5 4 3 2 1

For Helene Kann OCTOBER 1923

Torment of Life—Delight of Thought

Contents

Preface

The first and second editions of one thousand each appeared in 1909, the third in 1914. These were published by Albert Langen, Munich. Revision of the present edition followed in October 1923.

■

Setting out to put a book like this together from the *Fackel* had to involve more than just replenishing sold-out inventory, and the same goes for a reissue, especially when adding undated material; it always calls for another revision, to test how well the work has held up, across points in time and points of view, and at the bar of the conscience that determines artistic form, constantly reducing the leeway it permits words. A book explicitly embracing what is so routinely censured elsewhere, contradiction, would be entitled never to renounce it even in a single dictum. All the same, many of the sayings sprang from moods that were abstruse even at the time, or from an impetus long since impossible to recall; these plainly sacrificed worthy causes to the struggle against their unworthy adherents, and could not be allowed to stand. The impressions of those moments live on, but so does the feeling that forbids holding on to them amid the fundamentally altered conditions of our times, our greater experience of humanity at a furious boil. Letting them go certainly causes us less concern than the prospect of appearing to agree with a conservatism that survives this global destruction only as a malicious brat, wrenching concepts like democracy out of their cultural context, exposing them to intolerable misunderstanding and incomprehension. For justification of this authorial prerogative the reader is referred to the concluding remarks of "The World Destroyed by Black Magic." One-track minds, pressing on from a nonexistent starting point to a never-realized goal, may focus their worthless criticism on this editorial ingenuousness, and on the admission that among these phrases and passages there is plenty of opinion repugnant to the author's current views. This stage in his development has been left unretouched and unrepudiated, inasmuch as it reveals a consistent path to the present. Many of the dicta are stylistic high points the author has not surpassed since. Others could not evade his never-quieted urge for improvement, which confers pride on the moral and artistic responsibility at work in this editing, and will be made into a reproach only by the ninnies whose existence confirms the hopelessness of this book; as if their chance to compare versions had somehow ascended into the heavens. But if there is anywhere the author of the *Contradictions* knows he is above suspicion of contradiction, it is in everything he adduces against their personality type.

Dicta and Contradicta

One

1   Female sensuality is the primal spring where male spirituality draws renewal.

2   The sterile mind of the female nourishes the sterile lust of the male. But female lust nourishes the male mind, creates its works. Through everything she is not given, the female makes the male use his gifts. Books and paintings are created by womankind, though not by the woman who writes and paints herself. A work is brought to life: here the woman conceived what the man bore.

3   The true relation between the sexes is when the man confesses: my thoughts are never about anything but you, so they are always new!

4   Love in men may be merely a drive, but even the most thoughtless woman loves in the service of an idea. Even the woman that merely sacrifices to a stranger's drives is morally superior to the man who only serves his own.

5   Female personality is insubstantiality ennobled by unconsciousness.

6   Man has five senses, woman only one.

7   Male sexuality: functional; female: habitual. Male medical specialties are not called "male trouble."

8   Male joy—female suffering.

9   First God made man. But woman is a hysteron-proteron.

10 In female orthography the "ni" in "organism" is optional.

11 When a woman waits for a miracle, she is late for a rendezvous; the miracle was waiting for the woman. So unpunctual!

12 When a woman's senses fall silent, she starts demanding the man in the moon.

13 Is a woman really in the room before someone enters and sees her? Does womankind exist in itself?

14 Nothing is more unfathomable than the superficiality of women.

15 One quickly grasps the depths of a woman's mind; but it takes so long to push through to the surface!

16 For men the mirror merely indulges vanity; a woman needs it to be sure of her personality.

17 In every situation, in joy or sadness, outwardly and inwardly, a woman needs the mirror.

18 The eroticism of men is the sexuality of women.

19 Male superiority in the business of love is a paltry advantage, which gains nothing, only bludgeons the feminine nature. One should let each woman initiate one into the mysteries of sexual life.

20 The "seducer" who boasts of initiating women into the secrets of love: a foreigner who arrives at the train station, offering to show the tour guide the beauties of the town.

21 It is the realist politicians of love who extended to males the right to choose running mates.

22 They treat a woman like liquid refreshment. That the women are thirsty too is inadmissible.

23 One must regulate a beautiful woman's temperament so that moods can never harden into wrinkles. Jealousy prohibits our applying such secrets of spiritual cosmetology.

24 The forced lock with which sentimental femininity goes through life, and the other one, which closes itself back up as often as it permits itself to open: which is more intact, which more virginal?

25 A woman with a taste for men tastes only one.

26 The stronger a woman's personality, the more lightly she carries the burden of her "past." Pride goeth after the fall.

27 The ordinary female's genius for forgetting is not the same as the lady's talent for not remembering.

28 The sensual woman poses the greatest moral challenge; the moral woman serves a sensual craving. Bringing the unconscious to consciousness is heroism; dipping consciousness in the unconscious is finesse.

29 Even mental and moral qualities of women can arouse the worthless sexuality of men. It can be compromising to be seen on the street with a respectable woman; but conversing about literature with a young girl practically verges on exhibitionism.

30 When a woman makes a man wait, and he makes do with another, he is a beast. When a man makes a woman wait,

and she does not make do with another, she is hysterical. Phallus ex machina—the Redeemer.

31 Male desire is nothing worth contemplating. But when it rambles without direction, in search of a goal, it is truly an abomination against nature.

32 A hundred men become conscious of their poverty in the presence of one woman grown rich through squandering.

33 A woman has the advantage of always being able to say yes, but Nature has blocked it up with the man's corresponding disadvantage.

34 A man is at a disadvantage in not always being able to say "yes." For this he was compensated with enough sensitivity always to feel personally guilty about the inadequacies of Nature.

35 Feminine sexuality vanquishes all inhibitions of the senses, overcomes every feeling of disgust. Some wives would just as soon have bed without board.

36 Hamlet does not understand his mother: "Eyes without feeling, feeling without sight, Ears without hands or eyes, smelling sans all, Or but a sickly part of one true sense Could not so mope. O shame, where is thy blush?" A man cannot grasp this; the idea of a woman mating with King Claudius strikes him as an affront to him personally. He feels it is he who is laid "in the rank sweat of an enseamed bed," and his higher mental faculties are outraged. But here it is Shakespeare speaking, so Hamlet merely takes exception to the matron's age, where normally the "heyday in the blood" would be "tame," "waiting upon the judgment," with dis- criminating taste keeping the upper hand. He recognizes that in her youth a woman does not always have the choice between an Apollo and a patched-up scoundrel of a king; that sex and good taste generally wander separate paths; he "proclaim[s] no shame When the compulsive ardor gives the

charge." Were he not her son, he would concede even to the aging woman that the "devil . . . That thus hath cozened you at hoodman-blind" is just the sense of sex, which in the female—more than in the most sexual man—dims all the other senses and anesthetizes every principle.

37 Titania can embrace even a donkey. The Oberons never want to understand this; thanks to their lesser sexuality they would not be in a position to embrace a she-donkey. Which is why in love they themselves turn into donkeys.

38 Euphemism: she said about the singer, "His voice completely filled my ears!"

39 A pretty little girl hears a pawing noise at the wall of her room. She is afraid it is mice, and only becomes calm when she is told there is a stable next door and a horse is moving around. "Is it a stallion?" she asks, and goes to sleep.

40 The same girl could once say about someone who had pursued her: "He had a mouth that could kiss all by itself."

41 But the poet saw a rosebush. Some said it needed watering, but this the poet called a "satanic misconception." He thought it would suffice to pray daily to the rosebush: "Holy rosebush, noble, mysterious work of the Creator's art!"

42 The fetishist of the female soul, who counts the female body among those objects in the Museum Earth exhibit that one can only look at and not touch, preached: "a faithful and true feminine soul must be protected, guarded and defended by a such a rampart of inaccessibility and impregnability, dignity and spiritual nobility that Don Juan's gaze will lower and shyly turn aside! Then jealousy, this most dreadful disease of the male soul, will be banned, banished, vanquished!" But a perspective that totally discounts the desires of the desired and expects harm only from Don Juan, never from the female soul, leads us into an aesthetic doll's house,

whose peace depends on the chaste glance of the observer. Where is there room here to account for jealousy? A mere order not to touch the exhibited objects, and eroticism would become the objective evaluation of a posture, a nose, a hand. But in our world the dolls come to life, or become hysterical, depending on the strictness of the rules. Unapproachability becomes approach and impregnability a challenge. In a pinch even dignity can serve as a bait and spiritual nobility as a lasso.

43   How little you can rely on a woman who allows herself to be caught in the act of fidelity! Today she is true to you, tomorrow to another.

44   I only trust the woman who does not go about atoning for her sensual pleasures by conceiving spiritual children; who rinses away every experience in the douche of forgetfulness.

45   She said to herself: sleep with him, sure—just no intimacy!

46   In all the business of life the female stakes her sexuality. Sometimes even in love.

47   It shows how inessential and remote sexuality is from the male mind that even jealous men allow their wives to mingle freely at masked balls. They have forgotten how much they could once permit themselves there with other men's wives, and believe that public licentiousness has been repealed since their wedding. They sacrifice to their jealousy with their presence. They do not see this is a spur and not a rein. No jealous woman would let her husband wander off at the officers' ball.

48   The short memory of men is explained by their distance from sexuality, which dissolves in personality. The short memory of women is explained by their nearness to sexuality, in which personality dissolves.

49 A woman whose sensuality never falters, and a man constantly brilliant: two humane ideals that strike mankind as morbid.

50 The average female is sufficiently well armed in the struggle for existence. By giving her the ability not to feel, Nature has richly indemnified her for the inability to think.

51 A beautiful woman has understanding enough for one to talk to her about everything and with her about nothing.

52 When a woman utters witticisms she should wear a veil. Even then the silence of a beautiful visage is more stimulating.

53 The best women are those one speaks with least.

54 Women are there to make men wise up. This cannot happen if men cannot wise up to them, or if they are too wise.

55 Get used to dividing women into those that are already unconscious and those that need to be made that way. The first are loftier and commandeer one's thoughts. The others are more interesting and serve our pleasure. In the first case love is memorial and sacrifice; in the second, victory and prey.

56 "Dear hero, how much would I love you if I did not let you do new deeds?" Thus speaks the Wagnerian female. Such readiness would dissolve the hero's desire for exploits and women alike. For the desire for deeds stems from the desire for women. She should allow him not deeds but sex; then he will get on with the deeds. Wagner's words would match this psychology if the punctuation were changed (the German alliteration can stay): "Dear hero! How much would I love you if I did not let you? Do new deeds!"

57 A love affair, not without consequences. He bore the world a work.

58 Mothers get political preference over courtesans, who produce nothing, at best a genius or two.

59 Let us honor the harvest but love the landscape: it is more nourishing.

60 In the end all that matters is giving some thought to the problems of erotic life. Contradictions among one's results simply prove that one is right in each case. And contradictions with other thinkers still leave us closer to them than to those who have never reflected on the problems of erotic life.

61 Once you have made it from experience to thought, you can make it from thought to experience, enjoying the voluptuous fruits of knowledge. Blessed the man fate has granted women to whom he can effortlessly apply such thought!

62 How voluptuous to lie with a woman in the Procrustean bed of her worldview!

63 I am always strongly influenced by what I think of a woman.

64 A woman's valuation can never be just; but her over- or undervaluation is always in an earned direction.

65 When I can spread out a woman as I please, the credit belongs to the woman.

66 Women are either hollow suitcases or suitcases with inserts. The insert kind is more practical, but less fits inside. I prefer to pack my mind into the hollow kind, at the risk of getting it jumbled. The inserts disturb me, as if they were not-me. Culture has made women into camisouls, and one always carries along something that does not belong.

67 The playboy had discovered a similarity in her. He tended it; sat daily at her bedside and straightened her nose, to build up the similarity.—The aesthete had discovered a distinction in her. He tended it; sat daily at her bedside and praised the

holiness of her nose as an end in itself. He was thanking the Creator, but the playboy was a creator.

68   To immortalize the hand of a beautiful woman, as it were to amputate it from its living grace, you need that cruel disrespect for feminine beauty which only an aesthete can muster. Her hand need not be beautiful at all for a woman to hit like an act of God. There are women who blast into our erotic fantasy like a lightning bolt, shaking the ground and cleansing the air for thought.

69   The aesthete: She would be an ideal beauty, but—this hand! The playboy: "She is my ideal beauty, so all women must have this hand!"

70   All she lacked for perfect beauty was a flaw.

71   Beauty marks are the obstacles Eros uses to keep his courage in shape. Only women and aesthetes make faces about them.

72   A woman who cannot be ugly is not beautiful.

73   Some women are not beautiful, they just look that way.

74   Flawless beauty fails at just the moment that matters most.

75   Her features led an irregular life.

76   Big lips, big tips.

77   Cosmetology is female cosmology.

78   If women who paint themselves are inferior, then men with imagination are worthless.

79   Nudity is not eroticism, it is a subject for art class. The less a woman has on, the less she has on the higher sensuality.

80   A woman is more than just her exterior. The lingerie is also important.

81   Easier to forgive an ugly foot than an ugly stocking!

82 Women at least have their toilette. How are men to cover their emptiness?

83 "Thou unsubstantial air that I embrace!"—the confession of every sort of erotic refinement.

84 A woman should be water on a table top. You run your finger through it and it leaves behind no trace of where it was. That can be the most beautiful memory.

85 Sensuality can draw females into one another's arms. Imagination can do the same for men. Hetaerae and artists. "Abnormality" is when sensuality attracts a man, or imagination a woman, to the same sex. The man whose fantasy comes to include other men is loftier than the man drawn to women by mere sensuality. The woman whose sensuality comes to include other women is loftier than the woman who reaches men through mere imagination. The merely abnormal person may have talents but can never be a personality; while the "perversity" of the higher man and woman is the epitome of personality. Yet the law rages against both personality and morbidity, against worthiness and defectiveness alike. It punishes sensuality, which drives the complete woman into the arms of other women and the half-man into the arms of other men; and it punishes imagination, which drives the complete man into the arms of other men and the half-woman into the arms of other women.

86 *Sexus and Eros*

To Sexus it comes down to this:
Mr. is Mr. and Miss is Miss.

Eros fig leafs the private bits:
Miss becomes Mr. and Mr. Miss.

So beasties are hot for clarity,
But butterflies want ambiguity.

87 To the playboy the primary sexual characteristic is never attractive, always inhibiting—even the female organ. Thus he can gravitate to boys as well as women. The born homosexual is attracted by the male organ just as the "normal" man by the female parts as such. Jack the Ripper is more "normal" than Socrates.

88 The sexual man says: "If only this is a woman!" The erotic man: "If only this were a woman!"

89 Perversity is either a guilt incurred at conception or a right earned by accurate conceptions.

90 Whoever insists Xanthippe is more desirable than Alcibiades is a pig who thinks only of the sex difference.

91 You think you are talking with a man but you suddenly feel his judgments are coming from a uterus. This happens often enough for justice to demand that we stop differentiating people by the physiological characteristics they happen to have and switch to those they lack.

92 In literature we call it a metaphor when something "is not used in its literal sense."—Metaphors are the perversities of speech and perversities the metaphors of love.

93 The voyeur passes the strength test of natural sensibilities: the drive to see the woman with a man overcomes even the repugnancy of seeing the man with a woman.

94 Where might the greatness of women lie? In feeling. If I want a woman, I have a feeling. This I don't feel like. If it is she who wants me, then I don't get the feeling. And this too I don't feel like. So there is nothing left to do but withdraw, transform oneself from an accomplice to a witness. Or into a judge, who forces a confession of feeling. Or just switch off to women—if you started out capricious enough to assign them any value at all.

95 The erotic pecking order: The doer. The witness. The knower.

96 Erotic enjoyment is an obstacle course.

97 We love not the distant mistress but the distance.

98 When women return after a long absence one must have celebrations of nonrecognition.

99 Perversity is the gift of summing up imaginative values and sensations into an ideal.

100 What passes for normal is to venerate virginity in general but thirst for its destruction in particular cases.

101 What is a debauchee? Someone who has mind even in places where others have only body.

102 Dividing mankind into sadists and masochists is almost as foolish as dividing them into eaters and digesters. You have to ignore the odd cases; there are also people who digest better than they eat and vice versa. Thus one can safely assert that a healthy person has both perversions at his disposal. The ugliness here comes mainly from the words; the word taken from the name of the German novelist is particularly demeaning, and it is hard to savor things with unsavory names. In spite of this a man with artistic imagination manages to become a masochist in the presence of a real woman and a sadist in the presence of a fake one. He brutalizes the cultured monster out of her until the raw female comes to the surface. If it is already up there, the only thing left to do is venerate her.

103 If we are going to talk about the slave market of love, we should just face it: the slaves are the buyers. Once they have made the buy, human dignity is a thing of the past: they get happy. And how they toil in search of happiness, what a torment of joys! In the sweat of thy brow shalt thou find thy

pleasure. How the man plagues himself over love! But a woman with no grander name than Stella comes to grips with the most splendid social position.

104 Is "masochism" the inability to take pleasure without pain, or is it the ability to take pleasure from pain?

105 There is no unhappier creature under the sun than a fetishist who longs for a woman's shoe but has to make do with the whole woman.

106 Dancing-girls have their sexuality in their legs, tenors in their larynx. This is why women are fooled by tenors and men by dancing-girls.

107 Here is the difference between the sexes: men don't always fall for a small mouth, but women always fall for a big nose.

108 To maintain her health a woman would have to enlist her brain in the service of her drives. A fine utopia. If she has a brain to start with, she enlists her drives in its service and uses her sex to lasso the man's brain.

109 A beautiful but inauthentic flame of sensuality, when clear spirits catch fire!

110 Her eyebrows were dashes between thoughts—sometimes they curved up into musical ties of lust.

111 She permits him to tap at the gate of her lust, and allows a hint of the treasures she does not bestow. Meanwhile his dislike of waiting enriches her excitement: she takes alms from the beggar, saying, we don't give handouts here.

112 They pass the time with calculations: he finds the none-too-square root of her sensuality and she expotentiates him.

113 To prepare her for major intellectual surgery he anesthetized her with lust gas.

114   Consider the parallel between wit and eroticism. Both are children of repression, which dams the river of speech in one case and the flux of sexuality in the other. When it gushes unhindered, the sacred power of nature inspires awe: "the female is phenomenal at copulation."—Change just a few letters, put a little damper on the brain, and you enter the safe haven of a culture whose terrors cannot even fill us with admiration: "the lady is pheromonal at cogitation."

115   The true female betrays for pleasure's sake; the other kind takes pleasure for betrayal's sake.

116   Is she mournful or scornful? Is her reproach erotic or neurotic?

117   When the thief in the anecdote goes out stealing, the guard holds up a light for him. This situation is not unwelcome to womankind.

118   The man who warns a woman of danger is not a shrewd adviser.

119   The most confidential office: father-confessor for sins left uncommitted.

120   She had such delicate feelings of shame that she blushed when you caught her committing no sin.

121   Many a beauty marries a Jewish businessman out of sheer romanticism. She always hopes that the erotic robber baron will not be far behind the financial.

122   Cultured beauties have their own way of twisting up myths. Athena is born from the sea foam and Aphrodite springs in iron battle gear from the head of Cronus. Clarity does not return until one leg of Hercules' journey parts from the other.

123   Yet another heroic woman! If people could only see that the male virtues are illnesses in women!

124 Do-gooder women are often past the point of doing, er, good.

125 Do-gooder women represent a definite and particularly dangerous form of sublimated sexuality: Samaritiasis.

126 A woman's book may be good, but is it always the woman one should praise?

127 Female art: The face looks worse the better the verse.

128 A woman who uses vitriol is not incapable of reaching for ink.

129 A woman does not benefit from closer examination. This is an advantage she shares with every artwork one views as more than just a color study. Only women and painters are allowed to put each other under the microscope and evaluate their technique. Whoever else is disappointed by too close a look deserves what he gets. Such disappointments free him from the rosy chains of Eros. The connoisseur, by contrast, knows how to weave those chains from disillusion itself. The only woman who really disappoints him is one whose charms fade at a distance.

130 It can be a benefaction of the senses to stand now and then near a complex clockwork. Others see only the casing with the pretty metal sheet of numbers; they are content to know what hour has struck. Me, I wound the clock.

131 Even when two men are locked in an intellectual battle to the death, one can sometimes toss a woman a garland of flowers without the crowd noticing. But on second reading the pamphlet reveals itself to the sensitive eye as a love letter.

132 If women's absolute value can be measured, it surely has more to do with their general ability to bestow favors than with the worth of the particular objects they bestow them on. One cannot morally reproach a lightning bolt that crashes into a stump rather than an oak; yet there the beauty of

the spectacle depends on the dignity of the target, while the lightning bolts of sensuality shine brighter the further they reach down the social ladder. Only when the oak pleads in vain for the bolt's attention—then may the bolt be damned!

133 Many women would like to dream with men without sleeping with them. Let them be made expressly aware of the impossibility of this plan.

134 I enjoy carrying on a monologue with women, but a dialogue with myself is more stimulating.

135 Our delight in womankind hovers between the poles of boredom and discomfort. At these extremes they are either sisters of mercy or sisters without mercy.

136 Since keeping wild animals is illegal and I do not enjoy house pets, I prefer to remain unmarried.

137 Despite disillusionment we do not hold a grudge against our first mistress. Particularly when we met her in exercise class and it was beanpole-climbing.

138 A woman is sometimes quite a serviceable substitute for masturbation, though admittedly one demanding an excess of imagination.

139 Women are often a impediment to sexual satisfaction, but this makes them erotically usable.

140 Imagining, while in the act with a woman, that you are alone—this much imaginative exertion is unhealthy.

141 The beauty of the woman is a pleasant if unnecessary component of the enjoyment one finds in betrayal.

142 At night all cows are black, even the blondes.

143 A woman is entitled to be in denial about her minor flaws, such as a hunchback. But she should not deny she needs pince-nez.

144 An acquaintance told me he had conquered a woman by reading one of my works aloud. This I count one of my most splendid successes. It could all too easily have been me ending up in his fatal situation.

145 But withholding one's essence from women is not such a great pleasure either, I must say!

146 When a connoisseur of women falls in love, he resembles the doctor who gets infected at a patient's bedside. Professional hazard.

147 Only a man should take unhappy love to heart. A woman doing so looks so bad that one can understand her amatory misfortune.

148 A woman without a mirror and a man without self-confidence—how are they supposed to get by in this world?

149 Every woman looks larger from a distance than from close up. With women not only logic and ethics but optics too are upside down.

150 You may catch a woman in the act, but she will still have enough time to change the subject.

151 Nothing beats the fidelity of a woman who, no matter what the situation, remains firmly convinced that she is not betraying her husband.

152 What decent women find most impertinent is reaching up their consciousness.

153 Unfortunately the laws contain no sanctions against men who marry an innocent young girl on the pretext of seduction and then, when the victim has consented, want nothing more to do with her.

154 Some seduce women and leave them sitting there; others marry them and leave them lying there, and they are the more unscrupulous.

155 Many a man plays dirty tricks on a woman to avenge the sins his folly has committed against her.

156 With women society forces one to be either beggar or robber.

157 Greatest extravagance of feeling: If you knew what joy you give me when you come—you wouldn't do it, I know you wouldn't do it!

158 He wanted to condemn his mistress to freedom. That they will not put up with at all.

159 Full faith and credit is not just for government securities trading. They promise it in the meat markets too.

160 Masseurs agree that deeply bending the knee before a woman can do wonders.

161 All that matters in love is not appearing more of a fool than you have been made.

162 What I know won't hurt me.

163 A woman must be able to flirt skillfully enough for her husband to notice it. Otherwise he gets nothing from it at all.

164 The only man who truly loves a woman is one who also achieves a relationship with her lovers. In the beginning this always makes for the greatest suffering. But one can accustom oneself to anything, and the time comes when one grows jealous and cannot bear it if another lover is unfaithful.

165 It need not always be advantages of the male character or intellect that occasion a woman's infidelities. What is betrayed is above all the ludicrousness of the official position her owner occupies. Against that even physical advantages do not always offer a defense.

166 Just looking at a woman suffices to induce a profound contempt for her lover. But I would never care to burden her with the responsibility for this.

167 He would give her so much if she loved him for himself!

168 If you do not enjoy giving women presents, give it up. There are women who make the leaky jars of the Danaids look like strongboxes.

169 I cannot quickly free myself from the impression I have made on a woman.

170 He was so jealous that he felt the torments of the man he betrayed, and fell on the woman's throat.

171 Must we atone for the flaws the Creator left in females? Must we bleed just because every month they are reminded of their imperfection?

172 A woman does not feel the pains a man causes her. The man feels even these.

173 We have to get back to where one is done in not by the woman's indisposition but by her health.

174 A worthy man can never entertain such sublime thoughts about a worthless woman as a worthless man can about a worthy woman.

175 With a beauty, the most important task is overcoming her self-unconsciousness.

176 The hard-charging lover has nothing to lose. Another man stays away from women because the entire life he is nervously holding onto might drop out of his hand.

177 The origin of tragedy is a game of leapfrog.

178 A sleepwalker of love, who does not fall until someone calls out to her.

179 She had renounced the desire to reproduce, yet was born to new life every time she made love. She was made not to give birth but to be born.

180 First you see a woman other women resemble. Then you see another whose perspective resembles yours. But in the end there is none left and you see everything for yourself.

181 *Comparative Eroticism*

> Completion of the wondrous Venus icon:
> I take an eye from here, a mouth from there,
> From here a nose, from there round brows and hair.
> The present reincarnates what was bygone.
>
> Here wafts a scent, long since dispersed afar,
> Here sounds a tone long silenced in the vaults,
> And while I live death cannot hope to scar
> The Venus born from what my mind exalts.

182 It is not true that you cannot live without a woman. You just can't have had a life.

Two

183 The male of the species has tamed the wild flood of female sensuality into canals. Now it is no longer flooding the countryside. But no longer fertilizing it either.

184 The founders of norms turned the relation of the sexes upside down: they unchained the male sex while strapping the female into the corset of convention. This has dried up both grace and wit. There is still sensuality in the world, but it is no longer the triumphant unfurling of a primal essence, rather the wretched degeneration of a biological function.

185 Back when a woman's accessibility was still a virtue, the male spirit grew stronger. Today it eats its heart out at the perineum wall of a forbidden world. Mind and libido mate as before. But it is the women who have embraced mind, to titillate the daredevils.

186 How quickly men got to their day's work when they were still permitted to use the passage that stays open until lunar notice. The new housemaster of humanity will not tolerate this.

187 The "little woman" pushed out by the male has avenged herself. She has become a lady and has a "little man" for a house pet.

188 When Nature needs a haven from persecution, she escapes into perversity.

189 Decency is what is not unchaste but still brutally wounds my feelings of shame.

190 *Categories*

> Are they sinful or squeaky-clean?
> Alive or dead in the graveyard?
> Women you rank as fallen queens
> Or such as make nobody fall hard.

191 The Philistine despises the woman who has let him make love to her. How gladly one would concede his point if one could really blame the woman!

192 Moral responsibility is what a man lacks who demands it from women.

193 One unjust social death penalty necessitates another. Since society has locked up the whores in families, it has to lock up mothers in the bordellos. It's a logistics question.

194 Society needs women with bad characters. Those with no character at all are a worrisome element.

195 A beggar was condemned because he sat on a bench and "stared sadly." This world finds men suspicious when they look sad and women when they look jolly. Still it prefers the beggar to the prostitute; prostitutes are dishonest cripples, squeezing profit from the physical defect called beauty.

196 The dictionary says that *Aphrodite* means either the goddess of love or a worm.

197 How do these drips who force their agenda on us picture a "fallen" woman? Ninety out of a hundred such women would be perfectly good teachers for their children. Whore-housewives like these could scarcely be corrupted even by life in a nunnery.

198 For a coquette to strive for social honors is a sad humiliation; but at least she can compensate herself with secret pleasures. Much more despicable are the practices of those women who can cloak their secret respectability in a deceptive appearance of hedonism. They sponge off a social contempt they do not deserve, and that is the worst sort of social climbing.

199 Virtue is to vice as coal to diamonds.

200 Eroticism is the overcoming of obstacles. The most tempting and popular obstacle is morality.

201 How delightful it is when a girl forgets her good upbringing!

202 Virginity is the ideal of those who want to deflower.

203 The tragedy of Faust's Gretchen—what a fuss! The world stands still, heaven and hell open up, and the spheres sound the music of infinite regret. Not every girl takes the fall so hard!

204 Are the Germans still tying their dramatic knots with maidenheads?

205 For "mistress" we German-speakers say "beloved"; we no longer notice the height of pathos from which this word has descended into the lowlands of irony—deep beneath the respected neutral position of the unloved. The spirit of the

language wants the beloved mistress to be a "fallen" creature. But if beloved women were called "risen," our culture would soon fasten that name too in the clamp of scorn.

206 She cried: that bastard has put me in a blessed condition!

207 "Fallen women"? Whores fallen into marriage!

208 It is not done to marry a woman who had affairs beforehand. But it is the done thing to have an affair with a woman who married beforehand.

209 Love should spawn thoughts. In conventional speech the woman says: "What will you think of me?"

210 How a woman who could really live makes her lazy peace with the world: she foregoes personality in exchange for the concession of gallantry.

211 How powerful social mores are! Only a spider's web lies across the volcano, yet it refrains from erupting.

212 Surely a woman will not be so considerate toward society as always to commit the adulteries people attribute to her?

213 The triumph of public morality: a thief who has forced his way into a bedroom claims that his sense of shame has been injured, and by threatening to press vice charges he extorts a promise not to prosecute for breaking and entering.

214 Morality is a burglary tool, with the advantage that it is never left behind at the scene of the crime.

215 Society wants things this way: if a murder has occurred in a place where two people have met for sex, the two would rather bear the suspicion of murder than of fornication.

216 Custom demands that a sex murderer confess the murder but not the sex motive.

217 Fornicating with animals is forbidden; slaughtering animals is permitted. Has it occurred to anyone yet that slaughter might be a sex crime?

218 Immorality comes to light without deterring anyone. So much the more disturbing that the morality embodied in the State remains veiled, so it cannot set a good example. If people did not feel its presence now and then in the form of extortion, they would have no idea it even existed.

219 Asked whether he knew what "indecent" was, a little boy once answered: "Indecent is when someone is there." And the grown-up lawmaker would like to be there all the time!

220 Celibacy always takes its revenge. In one person it produces pimples, in another vice laws.

221 *Morality and criminality*

> We now can sleep in perfect ease,
> For out on lust's capacious moor
> Fierce statutes crinkle in the breeze,
> Ink scarecrows barring knave and whore.
>
> But warnings tempt those flighty friends;
> Our sleep is frightened by the sound;
> Libido triumphs yet again,
> The statute jeweled in her crown!

222 It would make an interesting statistic: how often the existence of commandments is the cause of their being broken. How many offenses are consequences of their penalties. It would be interesting to find out whether more children are defiled because of the age of consent or in spite of it.

223 The age of consent is the border most tempting to smugglers.

224 Punishments serve to deter the people who do not want to sin anyway.

225 A vice prosecution is the deliberate evolution of a private indecency into a public one, a murky background, against which the demonstrable guilt of the accused stands out in shining relief.

226 Scandal begins where the police leave off.

227 The vice squad makes itself guilty of turning privacy invasion into an official rite.

228 They judge so that they be not judged.

229 Quousque tandem, Cato, abutere patienta nostra!

230 In the Orient women have more freedom. They are allowed to be loved.

231 Male jealousy is a social convention, female prostitution a natural drive.

232 The core of prostitution is not that women are forced to swallow it but that they are able to stomach it, to put up with putting out.

233 Decent prostitution rests on the principle of monogamy.

234 The moral powers that be provided two monogamous life-styles that do justice to the female's secret talent for being prostituted and prostituting herself: mistress and pimp.

235 A mistress serves the sentence for her freedom in solitary confinement.

236 The immoral thing in a mistress is her fidelity to her owner.

237 The legal standing of the pimp in bourgeois society is not yet clear. He is society's excretion, since he respects what society rejects and he protects what it hunts. He is also capable of sacrificing for his principles; but when he demands others sacrifice for them, he fits himself into the frame of a social order that refuses forgiveness for a woman's prostitution but not for a man's corruption.

238 Male immorality triumphs over female amorality.

239 It makes sense that bourgeois society should regard the pimp with contempt, for he is the heroic counterpart of its entertainments. They are merely the worse Christians while he is the better devil. He is the anti-policeman who better protects the prostitute from the State than the State protects society from her. He is the last moral resort of a woman ruined for polite society. From society she could only grow rich; through him she becomes beautiful. When he robs her, she gets more out of it than she would from another's presents. Because he "sticks by her" he is even more despised than she; but this is merely a cloak for envy. Society has to pay for its fun; it receives goods for its money; but the call girl takes the money and keeps the fun too, all to give one man double the pleasure. Polite love is an economic matter, but here natural forces keep the books.

240 A horrifying materialism preaches at us that love and money have nothing to do with each other. The idealistic position at least admits a price level where true love begins: the same point where the man who wants to be loved for himself ceases to be jealous—though really this is where he could just as well begin: the playing field has shifted.

241 *Purification*

> Hookers fill you with contempt?
> A thief less nasty than a whore?
> Learn: not all love fees are rent.
> Cash can cause a true amour.

242 Not every man who takes money from a woman is entitled to fancy himself a player.

243 In old age a woman capable of love will enjoy the pleasures of a bawd. A frigid nature will merely rent rooms.

244 Bawds are the guardians of norms.

245 The pimp is a pillar to womankind. Without him the market in nice girls could easily collapse.

246 Woe to the poor girl who stumbles on the path to vice!

247 First safety from children, then child safety.

248 The moralists of sin are out to do away with the causes of childbirth. They say that performing abortions on lust is safe if you take all the precautions of scientific theology.

249 Science does not yet recognize the division of the sexes.

250 It is high time children enlightened their parents about the secrets of sexual life.

251 To hell with this chatter about the sexual education of youth! Even now a child gets more real education from a naughty classmate underlining the name "Hooker" than he does from a teacher explaining the whole thing as a state institution, important and complex, like taxation.

252 Love as a natural science! The prohibition against lust remains standing and now we are even forbidden the romanticism of taboo. But we request: if you must have Christianity, at least do it with incense, pipe organs and darkness, so the church offers a substitute for what it takes away.

253 How do people learn to swim? Someone warns them where the riptides are, and explains that water is a combination of hydrogen and oxygen.

254 Every conversation about sex is a sexual act. The ideal of the father enlightening his son about the facts of life has an aura of incest about it.

255 Morality is such a popular thing that any demagogue can preach it. But the preacher of immorality "violates ideals."

256 Only someone who has not experienced a problem will bring himself to write a lead article on it. But with this fear-

less generation touting sexual freedom throughout the marketplace, we have to protect the parents and teachers. Their unworldliness rests on experience.

257 The lewd are closer to the prude than immorality is to morality.

258 In sexual matters freedom does not need the comradeship of wickedness to dispose of its enemies.

259 Erotic enlightenment belongs in art, not education, but sometimes things have to be spelled out for illiterates. Persuading the illiterates is key, since they are the ones writing the vice laws.

260 For centuries humankind has branded the exercise of female rights with disgrace. So now it has to put up with the exercise of women's rights.

261 If you had recognized the rights of the female body, if you had repealed privates ownership of women as you repealed forced labor, women would never have come upon the absurd idea of disguising themselves as men in order to increase their value as women!

262 If only women's liberation aimed to dismiss female spotlessness as the mark of Cain, to show male blindness that there is such a thing as *prostitutio in integrum!*

263 The women are demanding both active and passive choice of running mates. Is this about having the right to choose any boyfriend they please, and being free of reproach when they allow themselves to be chosen by whomever? Heaven forbid: their agenda is political! But it is the men who have driven them to such despairing thoughts, and the men in turn will soon have no choice but to demand the right to menstruate.

264 When professionalism compels women to take it like a man, then men are naturally forced to take it like a woman. But

the goal of perfect competition between the sexes is flawed from the start anyway, during the period that no parliament can reschedule. Curses on a political order that sends women into the economic trenches even then! Let the blood spilled in that struggle be upon its head! She has enough to do defending herself against a world frozen with weapons. It is a cruel fraud to demand, on top of this, repayment of the sacrificial debt Nature demands.

265   So long as the women's movement continues, men should at least make it their duty to set aside gallantry. One can no longer risk offering a woman one's place on a tram, because one can never know whether one will offend her, short-change her claim on an equal share of life's unpleasantness. By contrast one should get used to treating feminists with every sort of courtesy and consideration.

266   When we start to study the female mind, we will begin to take an interest in male sensuality. What a prospect!

267   "Women's rights" are men's duties.

268   I heard a woman say admiringly of another: "There is something so feminine about her."

269   Women's liberation is making rapid advances. Only the sex murderers are not going along with the trend. There is a Belly-Slasher but still no Brain-Slasher.

270   Emancipated women are like fish who have come on land to escape the fishing rod. Even a rotten fisherman does not angle for rotten fish.

271   Satisfaction of the senses: the more disturbing Woman Question.

272   Beauty decays where virtue stays.

273   "An admirer of women is delighted to agree with your misogynistic arguments," I wrote to Otto Weininger after

reading his work. But how is it that a thinker who has risen to an understanding of the different female value system still cannot resist measuring both sexes with the same ethical and intellectual yardstick! That guarantees systematic outrage. But one thought calms it back down: where absence of both brains and inhibition makes for such grace, where lack of understanding and lack of feeling mate in an aesthetic union and the resultant of the worst qualities enchants the senses, then one can perhaps believe Nature does have a special plan—if one is allowed to believe Nature has plans at all.

274 Even in the life of pleasure there is a tragic conflict between personality and society and a sad conflict between inadequacy and professionalism. But the spiritually sovereign hetaera, who knows how to fight her way through life playing *grande amoureuse,* is just a construct of erotic wishes, trying to immortalize the drama of a sunset. The idea that a higher consciousness could guide even a dissolute life, could shore up sensuality even as it sublimates it, is something out of a novel. The clever woman is a dangerous player in the sexual chess game. Or she is sexless, a monster of calculation who on her wedding night performs integration without expotentiating her husband.

275 Where can the mind better quench its thirst than with feminine foolishness, hidden behind a witty face? When a woman is what she is supposed to appear, she wears out the male mind. The miracle of profound banality has been apparent to the world since Phryne; the world enjoys it but does not want to believe in it. Because the high minds of Greece wanted the company of hetaerae, the hetaerae have to have been high-minded women. Otherwise we would have no respect for the ancient Greeks. This is why cultural history has raised the cultural *niveau* of Athenian courtesans as best it could. Christian education has brought hysteria into the world and would like it to carry retroactive weight. But it

will have to learn to leave the maenads alone, and burn only the witches it has made of women today.

276 Womankind and music are now so ultrarefined that a cultured man need no longer be ashamed of being inspired by them. All that remains is for the meadows to become too hysterical for couples to lie on them.

277 Greek thinkers made do with whores. German military men cannot live without ladies.

278 The Christian zoo. A tame lioness sits in a cage. Many lions stand outside and look in with interest. The resistance of the bars whets their curiosity. Finally they break them down. The attendants wring their hands and flee.

279 Christianity suspended the customs barrier between intellect and sexuality. But sexual life saturated with intellect is a poor trade for intellectual life saturated with sexuality.

280 Christianity enriched the erotic mealtime with the hors d'oeuvres of curiosity and ruined it with the dessert of remorse.

281 Omne animal triste. That is Christian morality. Even there it is just post, not propter.

282 Stings of conscience are the sadistic impulses of Christianity.

283 In the struggle between nature and morals, perversity is either a trophy or a wound, depending on whether nature captured it or morality clobbered it.

284 *Christian Vowel Modification*

Frau Lewd disappeared from the world, married off to Herr Load of guilt.
Load is with her all day—he works nights; she said evenings she's home, but—she Lied.

285   The last sex act Christian culture permitted was the Judas kiss it gave the human spirit.

286   The joys of Tantalus belong in Christian mythology.

287   The spread of venereal infections caused the belief that lust is an infection.

288   Like Sancho Panza behind Don Quixote, so behind Christianity strides syphilis.

289   Mankind became hysterical in the middle ages because it had poorly repressed the sexual impressions of its Greek childhood.

290   Hysteria is the spilt milk of motherhood.

291   Religion and morality. Catholicism (kata and holos) is wholistic; Judaism is a Mosaic.

292   One exposes oneself today to plenty of unpleasantness just by saying about an artwork that it is a work of art. But one would be stoned to death if one said it of a woman's body, as loudly as would be necessary to restore it to new life. For morality wants it destroyed, and with words one can accord grace.

293   The times are troubled when the pathos of sensuality shrinks to mere gallantry.

294   Let it be a comfort to beauty that the walls that bar her from her source are the same walls where the mind bangs itself bloody. Both would have to trivialize themselves to gain admission.

295   Those who have provided the goblet of pleasure are dying of the poisoned cocktail Christian charity serves them.

296   It was a flight through the millennia, on the coldest night of winter, as she ran from a masquerade ball out onto the street, half naked, into the deepest Prater, with waiters, cava-

liers and coachmen in hot pursuit . . . a lung inflammation
and death brought her back to our century.

297   Facts valid for all eternity. That the primal energy of females
not only attracts and weeds out the weak, but animates and
rejuvenates the strong. That the best brains and greatest
characters have nourished themselves from this mental
weakness and lightheaded caprice. That the most powerful
rulers have made it through their years of erotic service in
one piece. And that in the divine design of the world, sensual pleasure and beauty are magic medicines, locked away as
poisons through the devilish designs of society.

298   When the princess danced with the coachmen to the music
of the barrel organ, she was so beautiful that the court
fainted.

Three

Human and Nearly Human

299 The Superman is a premature ideal, presupposing man.

300 The feeling one has about someone else's pleasure is always selfish. If we provided it ourselves, we claim half of it. But we feel the whole of the pleasure we watched someone else give him: half is envy, half jealousy.

301 Love thy neighbor as thyself. Because each of us is his own neighbor.

302 Whoever digs no pits for others falls into one himself.

303 Dogs are faithful, no doubt. But does this mean we should emulate them? After all, they are faithful to humans, not other dogs.

304 Gratitude as commonly understood is the readiness to smear yourself with ointment your whole life long because you once had lice.

305 I have been a supporter of the *point d'honneur* ever since I observed we have "unfinished business" to thank for our liberation from tedious company.

306 Not discussing evil deeds is part of good form. When some low fellow confides his intention to betray your friend, discretion is a point of honor.

307 Nothing is worth more to a military type than his word of honor. But if you buy in bulk you get a rebate.

308 A good Austrian folk idiom is "giving yourself a horseradish." Dignity makes people palatable, as horseradish does ham.

309 Honor is the appendix of the spiritual organism. Its function is unknown, but it can cause inflammations. One should calmly cut it out of people inclined to take offense.

310 Even stupidity has its sense of honor, and it defends itself against mockery even more vigorously than wickedness defends itself against blame; for wickedness knows its critics are right, but stupidity don't believe it.

311 How imperiously an idiot deals with time! He beguiles it or kills it. And time puts up with it; no one has ever heard of time beguiling or killing an idiot.

312 Society: everyone was there who was supposed to be there and who could not imagine Being having any purpose other than Being There.

313 Watch how our respectable gentlemen greet a woman with a "reputation." Their greetings unite the dismissive pride of pillars of society with the conspiratorial connoisseurship of porters. Both of which make you want to throttle them.

314 I heard a cheery German humorously declaim these words as a girl turned into a side street: "There she goes, the dirty slut!" It is not likely that a law will ever be passed permitting the shooting down of German men who with a single phrase have delivered complete proof of their uselessness here on earth.

315 A curse on the law! Most of my fellow men are sad consequences of a neglected abortion.

316 Nothing is more narrow-minded than chauvinism or racial hatred. To me all men are equal; there are flatheads everywhere and I despise them all equally. Who needs petty prejudices!

317 The unattractive thing about chauvinism is not so much the antipathy toward other nations as the love of one's own.

318 Religion, morality and patriotism are feelings that do not make themselves known until they are hurt. The idiom that says an easily offended person "likes" to take offense is right. Those feelings love nothing more than being irked, and they come right to life in grievances about the godless, the immoral, the rootless cosmopolitans. Removing your hat at holy communion is not half so satisfying as knocking the hats off people suffering from different beliefs or shortsightedness.

319 Officials will start being polite to the public only when the public decides to join the editorial staff of the daily papers. But the editors will start telling the public the truth only when it decides to join the bureaucracy.

320 The shrewdness of the police is the gift of regarding everyone as capable of theft, plus the lucky fact that many people's innocence cannot be proven.

321 A policeman usually resents it when you involve him in an official act.

322   All of city and society life rests on the tacit presumption that humans do not think. A head that is sometimes more than an impressionable hollow space has a hard time in this world.

323   Disavowal of intellectual life is a postulate of every society. Man is satisfied if you respect his skin and beneath it his so-called honor and so-called morality. His eye and ear must not be insulted, but their demands can be. The nose must pick up scents that it abhors, and when the sense of taste has prepared for food, the waiter comes after ten minutes and regrets that the kitchen is no longer serving. Every boor can gape at you; you have to tolerate impositions from every little drip, so long as he has asked whether you would mind his taking the extra seat; and just as you are hurrying to the desk to write down that you are living in a community of people who fancy themselves ethicists because they do not rip your wallet out of your pocket in the street, someone is guaranteed to cross your path asking for a light. Civilization is so proud of being obliging in this matter that no smoker dares answer the unwelcome accost with a curt No—nothing could better expose the mindlessness of the conventions we have established amongst ourselves. Prometheus got himself a light, from heaven. But even he was punished for it; Jupiter had him fettered to a cliff in the Caucasus, where a vulture pecked out his liver.

324   If a coachman's insistence that we ride with him collided only with our wish not to ride with him, life would be easy. But it sometimes collides with better thoughts and destroys them. Who thinks constantly about not riding?

325   When someone wants to address me, I keep hoping up to the last instant that he will be held back by the fear of compromising himself. But they are not intimidated.

326   I look through a window, and the panorama is soured by a fop's face. That is tragic. I have nothing against the existence of revolting faces. But why has optics set things up so

that a person can block out a forest? One can of course hold up a stick to cover up the person in turn. But even so one ends up shortchanged by the optical illusion. Thus light rays serve to augment misanthropy.

327 Given equal mindlessness, what matters is the difference in body mass. An idiot should not take up too much space.

328 "Ah was in Melk yestahday—dreahdful wetha," someone says to me suddenly on the train. "They say Eder dahd, the'mperial advasah," another says to me suddenly from the next table over. "Become a great man!" someone suddenly says to me on the tram in quite a different tone, pointing to someone who just climbed off, someone whose acquaintance he is obviously proud of. Without requesting it I find out what is going on in the inner life of my contemporaries. For me to behold their outer ugliness is not enough for them. We share life's journey for five minutes and I am supposed to be instructed in what moves them, makes them happy, disappoints them . . . this and only this is the content of our culture: the rapidity with which stupidity draws us into its vortex. We too have things that move us, uplift us, disappoint us: but in Melk, or at Eder's grave, or as regards the career of the great man, we are beentheredonethat. Our kind would never manage to create a similar effect on our fellow man. There I am standing still, because the sunset is the bloodiest red ever, and someone asks me for a light. I chase a train of thought that has just rolled around the corner, and behind me there is a shout: "Ta-xi." As long as a publican and a shoemaker are mere billboards, life is bearable. All right, for God's sake, let's memorize their faces. But suddenly they stand before us in the flesh, put a hand on our shoulder, and we collapse, like Don Juan when the statue comes to life.

329 Humans cogitate, near-humans navigate. They don't even think enough to think another person might think.

330 In personal interaction, intelligence disappoints, but stupidity is always productive. If you let it go to work on the intellect, it can create complete exhaustion, while wit has no enlivening influence on stupidity at all. A doctor should figure out why one falls apart physically in conversation with a dimwit, why the face goes pasty and the skin limp. One has lost maybe a pound, and that, like every forced diet, is disturbing.

331 One need not respond to every greeting. Least of all to those that merely express a request for favors. Greetings to critics are greetings of fear, no more high-minded than the greeting of taxi drivers, which is a greeting of hope: the greeters wish themselves good day. A mentality that twists friendly gestures into profiteering does not deserve the reward of causing physical discomfort.

332 Many people want to strike me dead. Others want to spend time chatting with me. The law protects me from the first group.

333 The city hall official is a curious species. If I dispatch my business in writing, he summons me. If I go in person the next time, he insists I submit it in writing. I am led to surmise that on the first occasion he wanted to meet me and on the second wanted my autograph.

334 To this great country we pledge our liberty and property, our wives and our lives! But our nerves?

335 I never sleep in the afternoon. Unless I had morning business in an Austrian office.

336 I would like to apply for a concession to hand-operate a guillotine. But the income taxes!

337 Sorrento, in August: For two weeks now I have heard not a single German word and understood not a single Italian one. One gets along with people quite well this way, every-

thing goes like clockwork and there is no possibility of friction and misunderstanding.

338   No place is more public than an elevator where they talk to you.

339   In the theater you have to sit where you see the public only as a black blob. Then they cannot get at you any more than they can the actor. Nothing is more disturbing than being able to differentiate individuals in a crowd.

340   If you want to study misanthropy at the source, sit in a restaurant near a theater and study the faces of the incoming hordes. How the tension remaining on the face of stupidity gradually eases and the flight from intelligence finds a new destination. Finally they are smacking their lips: that is the applause for the meal. Each one is embarrassed by himself, only happy in a chorus.

341   Where does distastefulness actually begin and where does it end? Why are there not eating closets as there are water closets? To eat publicly and digest privately—that is what suits these ladies and gentlemen! And yet nothing can match a menu for shamelessness.

342   Barbershop conversations are the incontrovertible proof that heads are there to hold hair.

343   When I get my hair cut I worry the barber will cut through one of my thoughts.

344   It is always one's own fault when one gets cut by the barber's razor. I, for example, cringe when the barber talks about politics; the others get nervous when he doesn't. In neither case is it his fault when someone gets cut.

345   Human aesthetic values seem designed solely to sucker us into shabby tricks. I treat them as a warning signal. I would gladly let myself be run over by a Viennese coachman, if he didn't do it so very nicely; and it would be my pleasure to

let an Italian innkeeper slit my throat, if he would just not open his eyes so dreamily. I prefer to put up with the discomforts of existence without aesthetic compensation; if something is going to aggravate me I do not want to hang around striking painterly poses.

346 Painterly and musical moments are arguments that dispense with all objections. And there are effects on the nerves which even the most contentious mind cannot resist. When all the bells are ringing I hug an alderman.

347 As a precaution, hysterical people should be anesthetized before operations performed on others. Also—to spare them any possible pain—before operations not performed.

348 Anesthesia: wounds without pain. Neurasthenia: pain without wounds.

349 The strongest force cannot compare with the energy many a man musters to defend his weaknesses.

350 The most incomprehensible babblers are the people who only use language to make themselves clear.

351 There are people who get hoarse when they have spent eight days in a row not saying a word to anyone.

352 What the common crowd resents most is your condescending when they cannot ascend.

353 Certainly the artist is The Other. But that is just why his appearance should match the others. He can only remain solitary if he disappears in the crowd. If he attracts attention to himself with some peculiarity, he debases himself and puts his persecutors on his trail. The more entitled the artist is to be different, the more necessary it is for him to clothe himself in the everyday, like a mime. A conspicuous appearance offers target practice to intoxicated philistinism; mocked everywhere else, it still fancies itself purposeful and exalted by comparison with longhaired eccentricity. The man in the

fool's coat gets a laugh even from the drunk the crowd laughs at. Purposely to neglect oneself in order to stand out; to wear dirty undies as a medal of honor for art and science; to shake an uncombed mane over the absurdities of society—a medieval ideal for wandering monks, long since set aside by the ruling classes, within the reach of every petty bourgeois. True bohemians do not concede the philistines even the pleasure of indignation, and true gypsies live by an unstolen clock. Poverty is still not a crime, but dirt is no longer an honor. "Mother Boulevard" disowns her sons, for these days even she is better groomed.

354 The most degenerate person is the one who is not entitled to be a stain on his family and a reject of society.

355 Only on special occasions does one don the garb of family feeling.

356 Family life is an intrusion into private life.

357 The phrase "family bonds" has an aftertaste of truth.

358 Today even a decent person—provided it never comes out—can make a name for himself.

359 A real man is someone who will never do the dirty deeds he is thought capable of. A half-man, someone never thought capable of the dirty deeds he does.

360 There are people who manage to unite worldly advantage with the moral cachet of victimhood.

361 Nothing is sadder than a base deed unrewarded. This species of wickedness should not pretend to itself afterward that it was art for art's sake.

362 It is better not to know how someone makes his living. Even economics should leave some room for imagination.

363 This suicide was committed in a fit of mental clarity. Even lovers of life sometimes contemplate suicide; there could

have been so many lives in this man that he had no qualms about giving one up. Suicide can be the bloodletting of a full-blooded nature. Whoever has feasted on life and wipes his mouth so calmly, to close it forever, rises above the common run of dinner companions. I cannot shake the suspicion that someone must be quite a fellow if today's world wrecks him. If something has fire, then given a light draft it will burn up. Only men without guts and women with brains can cope with the social order.

364   What a friend of good fellowship was the Bavarian king who sat alone in the theater! I would take it a step further and act the play myself.

365   Solitude would be an ideal state if you could choose which people to avoid.

366   The world is a prison where solitary confinement is preferable.

367   If I knew for certain that I would have to share eternity with certain people, I would prefer a solitary oblivion.

Four

The Press, Stupidity, Politics

368 Human arrangements need to become so perfect that they no longer disturb our reflections on the shortcomings of the divine.

369 Industrial life furthers the inner poetry artistic surroundings lame.

370 What? Mankind grows stupid for the sake of industrial progress, and we are not even supposed to put it to good use? We are supposed to hold dialogues with stupidity when we can flee it by car?

371 To the Philistine, art is fancy dress for everyday toil and trouble. He snaps at ornaments like a dog at sausage.

372 The common crowd tours "sites of interest." It asks whether the grave of Napoleon merits the interest of Mr. Sweeney.

373 The Philistine lives in a present well equipped with tourist attractions; the artist aspires to a past fitted out with all the comforts of the modern era.

374 Industrial development profits only the personality which realizes itself faster through exercise against the obstructions of the outside world. But the brains of the average man have not caught up with its hypertrophy. People have no idea yet what devastation the printing press wreaks. Aircraft are invented and still fantasy creeps along like a postal carriage. Automobile, telephone and gigantic editions of drivel—who can say what the generation after next will have for brains? Machines making for withdrawal from the fountain of nature; life supplanted by reading; all artistic possibilities absorbed by the spirit of facticity—the work will be completed astonishingly swiftly. In this sense we may be witnessing the incursion of an ice age. Meanwhile, let social policy go its own way, keep busy with its little tasks; let it administer public education and other surrogates and opiates. Passing the time until disintegration. Things have taken a turn unprecedented in any known historical epoch. Some do not yet feel this in every nerve, and will cheerfully carry on with the comfy division of history into antiquity, Middle Ages and modern times, until all at once they realize it has to go: the latest era has begun production of new machines for the maintenance of an old ethic. More has happened in the past thirty years than previously in three hundred. And one day humanity will have sacrificed itself to the great factories it built for its own relief.

375 We were complicated enough to build the machine, and we are too primitive to let it serve us. Global traffic travels in model trains of thought.

376 Social policy is the desperate surgical decision to remove corns from a cancer patient.

377 When the rafters are on fire, neither prayer nor floor scrub-
bing is any use, though prayer is more practical.

378 What syphilis has spared, the media will ravage. There will
be no way of knowing for certain what caused the brain rot
of the future.

379 Our culture consists of three drawers, two of which close
when the third is open: work, entertainment and teaching.
Chinese jugglers master the whole of life with one finger. We
will be a piece of cake for them. The Great Yellow Hope!

380 There is a dark continent that sends out discoverers.

381 Humanity, culture and freedom are goods more exquisite
than their cost in mere human blood, understanding and
dignity.

382 Democracy divides mankind into workers and idlers. It is
not set up to deal with people who have no time for work.

383 What is *X* up to? Keeping busy with Goethe's world spirit,
at the rushing loom of time.

384 Humanitarianism is a disappointment which sets in by a law
of nature, of physics. This is because liberalism is always putting its light under a bell jar, thinking it will burn in the air-
less space, when it will sooner burn in the storm of life.
When the oxygen is used up, the light goes out. But fortu-
nately the jar sits in phrase-water, whose level rises the instant the candle is extinguished. When you lift the jar, you
begin to sense the true qualities of liberalism. It stinks of
carbureted hydrogen.

385 All the words and deeds of today's so-called leading men
would have been impossible in the nurseries of earlier centuries. In the nurseries of today at least the argument of the
birch rod makes an impression. But human rights are the
flimsy playthings of grown-ups; they enjoy trampling them,

so they do not want them taken away. If one were allowed to use the whip, one would do it less often than one now wishes to. So where is the progress? Has the desire to whip been abolished? No, just the whip. In the age of slavery fear of the whip countered to the itch to use it. Today there is no counterweight, instead an extra incentive: the progressive pride of stupidity proclaiming its human rights. A splendid freedom: merely to avoid a whipping!

386   When human rights did not yet exist, the superior man had them all for himself. That was inhumane. Then equality was instituted, by disallowing the superior man's human rights.

387   When someone stands in the dock, there is no fact from his so-called past that cannot be used to create a momentary "unfavorable impression" and help law enforcement obtain the "motion" indexed in the court report. It is amazing how someone who has got himself mixed up in one indictment suddenly finds himself swarmed with them! Something that has stretched out over forty years acts as a living illustration when you project it onto the time scale of a trial. What went through the sieve of time achieves amplified actuality, as if it had all happened since the defendant's arrest. It casts light on the deed—with which it has nothing to do—but the deed casts light back on it too, so the defendant's character is always mirrored from two sides. This method is happily suited to judicial mediocrities and their lack of perspective. It is called shoving a lost soul under the dock.

388   Who is this: She is blind to justice, she makes eyes at power, and being near morality gives her thyrotoxicosis. And for the pretty eyes of this woman we sacrifice our freedom!

389   Merely exhorting judges to use the best of their knowledge and conscience is not enough. You would also have to have regulations placing lower limits on knowledge and upper limits on conscience.

390 Parliamentarianism is the barracking of political prostitution.

391 Politics has all the suspense of a thriller. The gesticulations of diplomacy present the comedy of states blackmailed by an international gang.

392 Politics is stage effect. When Shakespeare crossed the boards, the noise of weapons was still drowning out thought in every audience. The greatness of Bismarck, who creatively molded the political clay—and why should an artist's experience in the most earthly of affairs not turn into a masterwork?—is measured on a scale of theatrical action, of effect in entrances and exits. And if we Germans fear God and nothing else in the world, we respect even him not merely for his personality, rather for the sound of his thunder. Politics and theater: rhythm is everything, meaning is nothing.

393 Politics seems to me just as splendid a manner of dealing with the serious side of life as casting the Tarot, and since there are people who make a living at Tarot, the professional politician is a thoroughly comprehensible phenomenon. The more so in that he never wins except at the expense of those who do not play. But it is all right for the political bystander to pay, if patient spectating is his life. If there were no politics, then all the bourgeois would have to fill him would be his inner life, i.e., nothing.

394 In questions of politics memories of operetta are orientation enough. Characters like King Bobeche, Crown Prince Kasimir or General Kantschukoff have taught us most everything there is to say against absolutist government. If the phrasemongers' demand for politically engaged art is to have any meaning at all, it can refer only to operetta productions. These are vulnerable to the just criticism that for decades they have neglected the only human affairs that cannot be taken seriously: public affairs. The operetta is the form best suited to political developments, because its improbability

gives salvation to stupidity. For the rest of art to immerse itself in freshly baked events is a foolish demand; they are scorned even by satire. Satire can subsume the ludicrousness of politics generally, but the individual absurdities within politics are consummated beneath the *niveau* of real wit.

395   Who other than the politicians who commit them bothers to complain about the stupidities of politics? Are the clever parts of politics any cleverer?

396   "And makes us rather bear those ills we have, than fly to others that we know not of." Still I do not understand how justification of monarchy can go so far as enthusiasm.

397   Whenever a car goes by, a dog lodges his principled complaint though the futility of his cause is long since apparent. This is pure idealism, while the steadfastness of the liberal politician never barks at the car of state without selfish aims.

398   The pathos of German liberalism is a mixture of unprejudiced research and volunteer fire department.

399   The agitator's secret is to make himself as stupid as his audience, so they believe they are as clever as he.

400   Children play soldier. That makes sense. But why do soldiers play child?

401   Sport is a son of Progress, making its very own contribution to the stupefaction of the family.

402   The mission of the press is to spread culture while destroying the attention span.

403   Journalism only seems to serve the moment. In reality it destroys the mental receptiveness of posterity.

404   Ordinary duplication is progress insofar as it spreads noble consolidation.

405 When you reflect that the same technological achievement served both the *Critique of Pure Reason* and the reportage on the tour of the Vienna Men's Choral Society, all discontent leaves your breast and you praise the Creator's omnipotence.

406 Letting advertisers palm off X as Y—what newspaper will admit this typo?

407 A traveler in the Orient tells me that when it comes to religion there is no baksheesh. One could praise the Western liberal press in exactly the same terms.

408 One day I with my narrow horizon did not read a newspaper containing the following headlines: The secret 1869 negotiations between Austria, France and Italy. The Reform Movement in Persia. Croatian Departmental Head Named. The Porte vs. the Archbishop of Monastir . . . After not reading this newspaper I felt my horizon somewhat broadened.

409 The Providence of a godless era is the press. It has even exalted the belief in an omniscient and omnipresent power to a firm conviction.

410 Time and space have become Kantian categories of the journalistic Subject.

411 Newspapers have approximately the same relation to life as Tarot ladies to metaphysics.

412 The barber tells you the news when you just wanted a haircut. The journalist is witty when you just wanted news. Two types striving for higher things.

413 Humor magazines are proof that the Philistine is humorless. They go with the serious side of life, like drink with food. "Give me all the funny papers!" a sorrowful idiot orders the waiter; and he takes pains to have a smile appear on his face. From every corner of daily life he must have streaming at him the humor he lacks himself, and he would scorn even a

matchbook without a joke on the cover. I read on one such box: "Carpenter's boy (who has bought himself a sausage that happens to be wrapped in a poem): Very good! Now I can nourish my body with the sausage and my mind with the poem!" This sort of thing delights the Philistine; he sees no allusion to himself in the method of the carpenter's boy.

414   Spiritualism is the metaphysics of the neighborhood bar. It makes sense that a bar table should have to be rattled before anything spirited could appear, other than gin. The debunking of a medium is a change of pace for those who could otherwise not manage to debunk anything more than a card-sharper. Spiritualism is the madness of the thick-skinned. The only people who will fall prey to the fashionable urge to materialize spirits are those as far from spiritualizing matter as an elephant is from tightrope walking.

415   The military is hard up for recruits. Everyone wants to go into journalism.

416   If society is going to make businesses close on the Christian Sabbath for a "Sunday rest," the time should at least be used for reflection. Even reflection about the Sunday rest: people would grasp how necessary it is completely to automate public life. Who today enjoys a Sunday rest? Except for the salespeople, only the goods. For the buyers it is just an inconvenience. On Sunday the cigars rest in the cigar shop, fruit in the fruit shops and ham in the delicatessen. They have it made! But we would like to have it made ourselves and not have to go without cigars, fruit and ham during our Sunday off. If sacralizing Sunday meant going without pleasant things, the Sunday rest of the pleasant things would make sense. Since it merely aims to reduce the burden on the salespeople, it is antisocial, in effect if not intrinsically. Of course here in Austria it would be no surprise to see automats that would refuse to function on Sunday—Sunday rest, don't you know—and be out of order during the week.

417 For bakers and teachers to go on strike makes sense. But to refuse bodily or spiritual nourishment is grotesque. Unless one thinks it is adulterated. The most ridiculous thing in the world is a cultural hunger strike. I do endorse the barring of the universities; but it should not be via a strike. It should be out of desire, not spite.

418 When society wants to honor a prince, the schools are closed, work set aside and traffic stopped.

419 The orthodoxy of reason stupefies mankind more than any religion. So long as we can imagine Paradise, life is better then if we must live exclusively in the reality of a newspaper office. There we may honor the conviction that man is descended from the ape. But it would be a pity to have cured a madness that was also a work of art.

420 When a priest suddenly explains that he does not believe in Paradise and never will, it thrills the liberal press, whose editors are just as notoriously unwilling to give up their beliefs for anything. But wouldn't a pope of journalism immediately dismiss *a divinis* an employee who had the whim of announcing to the readers that he did believe in Paradise? The most repulsive sight the modern era has to offer: a priest possessed by the demon of reason, circled by the mongrels of the press, throwing them Adam's rib.

421 It is an enigma to me how a theologian can be praised because he has struggled his way to unbelief. The achievement that always struck me as most heroic and praiseworthy was struggling through to belief.

422 If you think belief is just another word for ignorance, you can shake your head demonstratively at dogmas. But it is pathetic to have to struggle to reach a position an assistant physics teacher has long since occupied.

423 The modernists are the only orthodox Catholics left. They even believe that the Church believes in the doctrines it pro-

claims, and that the bottom line is the faith of those responsible for promulgating them.

424   Clericalism is the confession that the other person is irreligious.

425   In Echternach, in Luxembourg, they have to this day so-called jumping processions. The farm animals once got St. Vitus' dance, and the local farmers vowed to follow suit in honor of St. Willibrord. These days neither man nor beast recalls the origins of the odd ceremony, but the Echternachers are faithful about it, and if habit retains its power, perhaps the beasts will one day jump again for St. Willibrord. For now it is still people, about 50,000 of them, who each Whitsuntide jump "three steps forward, two steps back." The priests do not join the jumping, they just watch. The spectacle does not altogether satisfy them: they would rather see two steps forward and three steps back.

426   In Lourdes you can be cured. But what magic is supposed to emanate from a nerve specialist?

427   Psychiatrists are to psychologists as astrologers to astronomers. The astrological streak has always been there in psychiatry. First our actions were determined by the position of the heavenly bodies. Then the stars of our fate were in our breast. Then came the theory of inheritance. Now the stars of fate are at the breast of our wet nurse; the whole tone of life is supposedly set by whether she pleased the suckling babe. We make childhood sexual impressions responsible for everything that happens later. It was worthy to clear away the belief that sexuality and adult education begin at the same time. But one should not exaggerate anything. Even if the time is past when science chastely abstained from empirical knowledge, that does not mean one should give in unrestrainedly to the pleasure of sexual research. "My father," sneers Gloucester's bastard, "compounded with my mother under the Dragon's Tail, and my nativity was under Ursa

Major, so that it follows . . ." Still, it was more beautiful to
be dependent on the sun, moon and stars than on the Fates
of intellectualism!

428 The old science denied recognition to the adult sex drive.
The new one asserts that babies at stool already feel lust.
The old model was better. At least the parties involved were
capable of specific assertions to the contrary.

429 The new spiritual researchers say that anything and everything traces back to sex. For instance, you could explain
their methods as father-confessor eroticism.

430 Neurologists who pathologize genius should have their
skulls crushed with the geniuses' Complete Works. One
should do the same with the representatives of a humanitarianism that complains about vivisection of guinea pigs while
permitting experimental abuse of artworks. All those who
offer to prove that immortality is rooted in paranoia, all the
rationalistic helpers of the average man, who reassure him
about his lack of inclination to works of wit and fantasy—
grind your heel into their face whenever you get hold of
them. Shakespeare, deranged? Then mankind sinks on its
knees, terrified for its health, and begs the Creator for more
derangement!

431 Neural pathology: if someone lacks nothing, the best way to
cure him of this condition is to tell him what disease he has.

432 Nerve doctors make the patient into a doctoral candidate.
He acquires a self-confidence of the unconscious, uplifting
but not exactly promising. Instead of chasing him away
from his burning problems, he is confined to roast in them;
instead of distraction from his troubles psychoanalysis produces an intimacy with them, a kind of pride in his symptoms, which at best puts the patient in a position to under-
take equally unsuccessful cures on others. All in all a method
which manifestly makes laymen into experts faster than it

heals the sick, since the active ingredient in its prescription is the disease itself, self-observation—hardly a spiritual serum.

433   Medicine is so lacking in perspective when it describes symptoms! They always match the patient's imaginary suffering.

434   Momo the bogey man is an indispensable pedagogic aid in German family life. To frighten the grown-ups you have to threaten to have them committed.

435   Psychiatrists can recognize madmen by the visible agitation they display after involuntary commitment.

436   The difference between psychiatrists and other disturbed people is the ratio of convex and concave folly.

437   Pedants can still read only from right to left: they see "live" as "evil."

438   Science does not bridge the chasms of thought, it simply stands as a warning sign before them. Those who ignore it have only themselves to blame.

439   Vacillating through life in the grip of madness—such a man might in the end stride more uprightly than the initiate groping his way along the rim of the abyss.

440   Religion is called the constrained worldview. But it is constrained by the cosmos, while liberalism is free in one precinct.

441   When an epidemic of stupidity breaks out in a town, it must be declared contaminated. Every case must be revealed to the authorities: some numskull could so easily have walked in and out of a house where there are children. In such times the best policy is not to open the schools, as some might think, but to close them.

442   It is worth recognizing that education is the epitome of what one has forgotten. Beyond this it is a disease, a burden on the educated person's environment. It is ridiculous to

reform the dead languages out of the schools on the grounds that no one needs them in practical life. The day to abolish them would be the day they became practical. Certainly they do not help you quiz your way through the tourist sites of Rome and Athens. But they sow in us the ability to imagine them. School is a poor place to amass practical knowledge. But mathematics cleanses the neural pathways, and even when one must swot up on dates one promptly forgets after graduation, one is not doing something useless. The only misguided thing is German language class. But in exchange one learns Latin, which still has a special value. Do well in German and you become a German military man. Do badly in German but well in Latin and you might become a German author. What school can do is create that vapor of living things that draws an individuality out of its shell. If a pupil still knows years later exactly which act of which classical drama a quote comes from, the school has failed. If he knows where it might have come from, he is truly educated and the school has achieved its goal perfectly.

443 The point was to abolish not the flogging-stick but rather the teacher who applied it badly. Like all humanitarian patchwork, such school reform is a victory over the imagination. The same teachers who until now could not even form an opinion without the help of a textbook will now have to immerse themselves lovingly in the individuality of each pupil. Humanitarianism vanquished the nightmarish terror that you would "get it" over the teacher's knee, but making life danger-free will make it even less bearable. Between "excellent" and "quite unsatisfactory" there was elbow room for romantic experiences. Childhood trophies cost me some sweat which I do not want to wipe from my memory. The hopeful spur has disappeared along with the cruel goad. The schoolboy has as little ambition as a smiling man of the world, and steps unprepared into the struggles of life. Previously his character had anticipated them without damaging

itself, as an inoculated body does smallpox. He had tasted all the dangers of life, all the way up to suicide. Instead of driving away the teachers who let toy dangers become all too real, the experts prescribe the seriousness of a quiet life. Pupils used to experience school; now they just have to let it shape them. The delight has been chased away along with the fright, and the young mind stands before the chalkboard of a Protestant Heaven. The schoolboy suicides motivated by the stupidity of teachers and parents will disappear; but boredom remains as a legitimate suicide motive.

444 A comprehensive education is a well-stocked pharmacy; but there is no guarantee that a sniffle will not be treated with cyanide.

445 When a man passes for universally educated, he may still have one great chance in life: that he really isn't.

446 Is there really no protection against the typo that turns every erudition from "stupid" to "stupendous"?

447 Lots of knowledge fits into a hollow head.

448 Culture hangs on his body like a dress on a mannequin. Such scholars are at best supermodels of progressive fashion.

449 Men of science! People say many things about science, most of them wrong.

450 The value of education makes itself clearest when educated people start talking about a problem lying outside their specialty.

451 It is an old question whether Goethe or Schiller is more popular among Germans. Yet Schiller's phrase "This low-life's name is Franz?" has not had anything like the profound effect destined for the more general formulation Goethe's Götz uses on the captain. Since for decades scarcely a day has gone by in German courts without the report stating the defendant "directed at the plaintiff the

well-known challenge from Goethe's *Götz*," it is clear that Goethe's posthumous fame is more firmly grounded. The honor in which the populace holds its geniuses is clear not only in its immediate discovery of the passage most delectable to German tongues, but also in no one being uncultured enough anymore to use the phrase without invoking Goethe's name.

452   Thanks to mass-produced lingerie, higher German thought has taken the path through unity to depravity.

453   The Germans sit at the table of a culture whose head chef is Blowhard.

454   Whether in manufacturing, in literature, in law, music, medicine or drama: in the sacred world of the mind there is no escape from the ubiquitous power of the military.

455   Originally groomed for the business world, he actually ended up dedicating himself to literature.

456   The new Siegfried. The immeasurable change from the image once bound up with the name demonstrates the superiority of its present holder. Every inch of his skin is calloused, and he knows better than his predecessor where to find the golden horde: he has the map.

457   The time is coming when the golden fleece will be taken from the golden calf!

458   If there were a medal for Leniency in Human Rights, our contemporaries would run themselves raw to get it. What holds them together as a society is their stripes, and their disenfranchised are martyrs who have received no crosses, maltese or otherwise. It is the old song of stupidity, which craves any distinction, even a star falling on its head in recognition of its contribution to the end of the world.

459   People often dream they can fly. Now all mankind dreams it: but it talks too much in its sleep.

460   Since mankind began attempting the conquest of the air, the earth too is mobilizing.

461   Nature is urging us to think twice about a way of life focused on externals. A cosmic dissatisfaction is making itself known everywhere: summer snow and winter heat are staging demonstrations against the materialism that makes existence into a Procrustean bed, treats spiritual illnesses as stomach aches and wants to deface nature wherever it sees her features: in the wild, in woman, in the artist. A world that would tolerate its own demise if only it were allowed to watch it in the cinema is not going to be intimidated by the incomprehensible. But our sort construes an earthquake without further ado as a protest against the achievements of progress, and does not doubt for a moment the possibility that an excess of human stupidity could outrage the elements.

462   After the downfall of Messina. It calms one somewhat to feel this rage of nature against civilization as a tame criticism of the devastation civilization has wreaked on nature. Look what it has made of the forests, of the women! Nature could be appeased with a magnificent renewal of our allegiance, a sacrificial festival of good works. Christian love, forget to be Christian! Samaritans male and female, come on! All you who are just doing a distasteful duty—come! One can replenish whole peoples in a single day. In one day one can gather riches and build cities. One day to celebrate life in this world all full of dirges!

463   The task of religion: to comfort men on their way to the gallows. The task of politics: to make them sick of life. The task of humanitarianism: to shorten their time on death row, while poisoning their last meal.

Five

The Artist

464 Grasping the world with a glance is art. Amazing how much fits into an eye!

465 Personality has it, talent is it.

466 Having talent—being a talent. These are always confused.

467 Talent is a boy awoken. Personality sleeps long and wakes of its own accord, so it thrives more.

468 When a worldview begins to shed its skin under the penetrating rays of personality, it suggests a sound constitution.

469 Personalities have it bad. The masses see only the surfaces where contradictions etch themselves. But these represent a deeper level where they converge.

470 The imitator pursues the traces of the original, hoping the secret of its individuality will somehow reveal itself. But the closer he gets to the secret, the further he gets from the possibility of using it.

471   There is no lust that can compare with the peak pleasure of spiritual production, and no sorrow comparable with the state the artist sinks into after a work is finished. Invariably the self-confidence of the unconscious creates the first and hence the best work. When it is done, the uncertainty of consciousness sees it is the last and hence the worst. When you are this dejected, every cheap critical jab leaves a dent. A mentality that can follow artistic creation merely into sobriety and not into enjoyment is a real curse. They know nothing of lust who only know it precedes sorrow.

472   Mental work resembles the act of love so much that there too one involuntarily obeys the conventions of sexual life. One is discreet, and when a woman comes visiting while one is at work, one does not let her in, to avoid an embarrassing meeting. The Philistine is busy courting a woman, the artist courts a work.

473   A good stylist at work should feel the pleasure of a Narcissus. He must be able to see his work so objectively that he catches himself feeling envious and needs memory to remind him he himself is the creator. In short, he must maintain that highest objectivity which the world calls vanity.

474   The thought of artworks as nourishment for the philistine appetite frightens me awake at night. Being digested by the bourgeois is a revolting prospect. But lying in his stomach is none too tempting either. Thus it is perhaps best not to serve oneself to him at all.

475   There grows no herb that can cure the curse of creative compulsion.

476   A productive person cannot absorb much information. A well-read poet arouses suspicion.

477   When one's policy on external impressions is "keep out," it proves one's thoughts are not on strike.

478 I saw a poet in the meadow chasing a butterfly. He set his net on a bench where a boy was reading a book. Too bad the roles are generally reversed.

479 A poet who reads: like watching a cook eat.

480 Why should one artist comprehend another? Does Vesuvius respect Aetna? At best there could be a feminine relationship of jealous comparison: who spews better?

481 Works of art are superfluous. It is necessary to make them, but not to show them. If a man has art in himself he does not need an outside stimulus. If he does not he sees only the stimulus. The artist forces himself on the one and prostitutes himself to the other. In either case he should be ashamed.

482 Art serves to rinse out our eyes.

483 When things go astray on the world stage, the orchestra falls in with them.

484 The Philistine is not in a position to supply his own spiritual uplift, and needs to be reminded incessantly of life's beauties. Even for love he needs an instruction manual.

485 Some people find X beautiful, others Y. But they have to "find" it. No one wants to search for it.

486 For the Philistine time passes. For the artist it masses.

487 There are two types of art lover. The first praises the good because it is good and faults the bad because it is bad. The others fault the good because it is good and praise the bad because it is bad. They are easy to tell apart, since the first does not exist. So one could easily recognize them, were it not for a third category: those who praise the good although it is good and fault the bad even though it is bad. It is to this dangerous type that we owe all the disorder in artistic matters. Their instinct directs them to choose the wrong thing, but they deliberately choose the right thing

instead, for reasons that lie outside artistic sensibility. The artist could live without the snobbery that exalts him, but scarcely without the stupidity that dismisses him.

488 An artist who makes concessions achieves no more than a traveler who tries to make himself understood abroad by speaking pidgin English.

489 A snob is unreliable. The work he praises might be good.

490 Not everything attended by a deadly conspiracy of silence is alive.

491 Criticism does not always demonstrate its customary incisiveness: it often ignores the most worthless ephemera.

492 In earlier times the cobbler had a personal relation to his boots; today the poet has none to his experiences.

493 There are no more producers, only sales reps.

494 They forego homegrown art and prize whatever the marketplace craves.

495 Talent is often a character defect.

496 There is one sort of talent whose exercise should be forbidden by law. It the one that has brought into the world all the evil which hinders cultural development by intellectually contaminating spiritual life.

497 Since Heine, verses are cobbled together on the boot-tree "a talent but not a character." But I do not draw such fine distinctions! A talent, because not a character!

498 The talent that flutters through the world with no center of gravity is worrisome because it gives sweet refreshment to the Philistine's animosity toward everything authentic. One Sunday magazine buries a dozen works of art.

499 Art is so willful that it does not consider skilled fingers and elbows proofs of ability.

500 Artists have the right to be modest and the duty to be vain.

501 A man may be happy to do without the praise of the mob, but he will not deny himself the opportunity to become his own disciple.

502 The Philistine gets bored and seeks things that will not bore him. Things bore the artist, but he never gets bored.

503 To my imagination she is a gracious princess—to my reason, a scullery maid. The artist lets both roles play concurrently. The Philistine is disappointed and retracts the first.

504 Music cleanses the shores of thought. Only people with no mainland dwell in the world of music. The easiest melody awakens thoughts, like the easiest woman. The man with no thoughts seeks them in music and womankind. The new music is a woman who compensates for her natural flaws by fully mastering Sanskrit.

505 I refuse to be dissolved in music. Music worthy of the name must dissolve in me.

506 What is the Ninth Symphony compared with a popular tune played by a barrel organ and a memory!

507 Music I make to the clattering of a railway trip or the rumbling of a carriage can transport me higher than all philharmonic piety.

508 A barrel organ in the courtyard disturbs the musician and gladdens the poet.

509 Noise never causes complete irritation, for deep underneath it is music's relation.

510 Passions can make music. But only wordless music. Which is why opera is nonsense. It posits the real world and fills it up with people who sing during jealous scenes, headache, and declarations of war, and cannot forego coloratura even on their deathbed. It reduces itself *ad absurdum* through the

incongruity between the greatest seriousness humanly possible and the curious custom of singing. In operetta the absurdity is there from the beginning. It posits a world where causality is suspended, in accordance with the laws of Chaos that created and merrily animate its world, with singing accredited as a means of communication. Operetta is self-evidently nonsensical, so it does not outrage one's reason. It is plausible for operetta conspirators to sing, but in opera the conspirators are in earnest and damage the seriousness of their intent with unmotivated singing. Operetta nonsense is romanticism. Here music's function of dissolving the cramp of life, reinvigorating mental activity through relaxation, couples with an irresponsible liveliness which makes the confusion onstage suggest our real-life follies. The essence of operetta is an intoxication giving birth to thoughts; sobriety goes away empty-handed. But presupposing a romantic world becomes ever more difficult in a real world which allows fewer presuppositions every day. Hence operetta must be rationalized. It denies the romanticism of its origins and pays homage to the mentality of the *commis voyageur.* The source of pure operetta idiocy is the demand that the operetta withstand the test of pure reason. Nowadays there is no more bursting into song from Bobeche and Sparadrap, from the shepherd princes and princesses of Trebizonde, from the dread alchemists with their poison powders made of confectioners' sugar. There are no more royal families that can be carried away into musical excesses by the mere word *Drum,* no more off-key courtiers crushed by a tyrant's merest breath. Instead attaches and lieutenants matter-of-factly convey their message to their lady partners in tone language. Psychology is the ultima ratio of incompetence, and so the operetta also had to be psychologized. But when the nonsense was in full bloom, it was educational, in that the Graces were the artistic measure of its foolishness; operetta nonsense could be credited with enhancing life. An orchestral joke in Offenbach's *Bluebeard* taught me more sensitivity than a hundred operas. It is only now that the genre has taken to reason and donned a dinner jacket that it will earn the contempt aesthetics has always shown it.

511 I can imagine a young person getting more decisive impressions from the works of Offenbach, heard in a summer theater, than from the classics pedagogy presses him to absorb without understanding them. They could perhaps spur his imagination to master the hard work of forming from the "beautiful Helen" the pictures of those heroes the Iliad has not yet revealed to him. Perhaps the caricature of the gods can gain him entry to the true Olympus.

512 Opera: Consistent characters and realistic events are advantages which do not require a musical complement.

513 Musical theater is the profanation of direct poetic thought and intrinsic musical seriousness. Instead of using so-called entertainment to introduce indirectly the effects "anthologies" lay claim to, it puts the brakes on them. The latest comedian's drive for publicity brings literary art to naught, and the devotional exercises of a Wagnerian opera are histrionic nonsense.

514 In opera music mocks theater, and the natural parody which arises from juxtaposing two forms makes a mockery of even the most effectual resolve to create a "total work of art." Action and song can meld into such a work only in operetta, which presupposes folly.

515 Nothing is more senseless than the call for dancing girls without tricots: the demand of that literary vegetarianism which so fundamentally misunderstands art and nature and which, by identifying one with the other, creates the effects it wants to abolish. Without makeup the actor plays paleface before an audience of Indians; unadorned dialect is an affectation, and the nudity of the dancing girl is a costume.

516 Homeopathy is the rage in the arts too.

517   The favorite confusion of theater critics is between the personality which cannot but express itself and the inadequacy which cannot express anything but itself. Both are "nature." There was a time when we were lucky enough to have a few special people treading the boards before us every evening. Their artistry could never transform them so much that we could have failed to recognize them as special people. But now we are told that individuality has differentiated itself: that actors one recognizes immediately by their stuttering or squinting are also individualities. Such criticism is at a loss when faced with two Falstaffs: should it prefer an overflowing spirit playing itself, or a plausible paunch?

518   In the theater one must not confuse the nature of a personality with the naturalness of a person.

519   The new art of theater: dilettantes without stage fright.

520   Actors for effect have been supplanted by actors for defect.

521   There are personal and objective actors.

522   The art of acting should make itself independent again. The actor is not the servant of the dramatist, rather the dramatist of the actor. Admittedly Shakespeare is too good for this to apply; Wildenbruch would suffice. The stage belongs to the actor; the dramatist should just deliver the opportunity. If he does more, he takes from the actor what is his. For centuries, the poetry that belongs to the book has quite deliberately sponged off the stage. It has fled the reader's imaginative poverty to speculate on the viewer's. At long last it should be ashamed of the popular effects it has lowered itself to. The public has never yet grasped a Shakespearean thought, it has only let itself be tranquilized by the pleasant subject or by the rhythm, which can also be the vehicle for nonsense. "Life's lack of understanding / With heavy heart in joy to taste / Is virtue, insight . . ." with this line a tragic actor can so shatter the house that everyone thinks it is by

Sophocles rather than Thuemmel. Praise to the actor who emphasizes his creative tyranny in his choice of even unliterary occasions!

523 True actors accept from the author only cues, not specific words. To them a theater piece is not poetry but a field of play.

524 What shows the actor's magnificentrality in the theater is that the success of the dramatist rests on poetic alterations undertaken by the actor. The actor earns the royalties.

525 I do not trust the printing press when I turn my written work over to it. How can a dramatist rely on the mouth of an actor!

526 The personality distance between actors and playwrights is most conspicuous when the actor plays a playwright. He is not credible. What works for him is heroes and everyday people.

527 The only art the public has some judgment about is the art of theater. As individuals the spectators—the critics, above all—talk nonsense. But taken together they are right. The reverse holds for literature.

528 An actor interested in literature? A literary man doesn't even belong in the orchestra stalls!

529 When the actor playing the father in *Henry IV* stresses the word *father* in the sentence "Thy wish was father, Harry, to that thought," he can move the public to tears. Another actor who stresses the word *wish* as the sense demands is merely not understood. This example shows how hopelessly language struggles in the theater against the thespian element, only to draw life from defeat in the end. The drama always asserts its stageworthiness in spite of thought or in contrast with it. Even with a joke the public's palate is tickled merely by the content. The more physicality the joke

has, the more it offers the public to hold on to, the easier it has it. This is why Nestroy's intellectual humor is less effective than the equivalent situation in his French model. A bon mot like "in a castle in the air even the janitor's apartment has a view of paradise" falls flat. Unless an introduction from the friendly emcee helps it get a little rise.

530 A dramatic work of art has no business on the stage. The theatrical effect of a drama should go as far as wanting to see it performed: anything more destroys the artistic effect. The most fantastic performance is the one in the reader's fantasy.

531 The painter too should be treated onstage as someone not employed there. Literary and painterly theater is an amputated corpse, on which drunken doctors have placed the arm of an ape and the leg of a dog. When poets and painters take squatter's rights on the stage, then the only place left to look for good acting is in libraries and galleries. Perhaps the buffoons of culture have already naturalized them there.

532 Just once I would like to read: This new production has presented everything ever gone beyond.

533 In earlier times set designs were cardboard and the actors were real. Now the set designs are completely convincing but the actors are cardboard.

534 Modern directors do not know that one must *see* the darkness onstage.

535 The scene is so naturalistic that it makes real clocks chime. That is why the time passes so slowly.

536 One suspects that all of modern art subsists on the extraneous. The theater of imperfections, the music of interruptions.

537 If you want to judge an actress you must measure her with the yardstick of womankind. Her face is a better touchstone of talent than her declamation, makeup makes the woman

nothing more than imagination does, and the rostrum serves for prostitution in the highest sense. Take the case of the heroine: she can create only from the tragic conflict with which the social world threatens what is most feminine. She remains in the straight mainline of female sensibilities. The hysterical woman sets out on a side path to the stage. The reviewer considers it praise when he writes of an actress that her countenance emits no "siren call of the senses; while the doglike pug nose of R. charmed an entire generation." This is because "the animal sexuality of her crafty coquette face got on people's nerves." How true! But for that very reason R. is a greater actress than any of these unhappy creatures whose so-called soul consists in exploiting their feminagity. The question of an actress's beauty seems tactless to the well-informed Thebans. But her charms are not a sleazy fact of her private life, they are a condition of her art. "With a little walk-on actress," says that reviewer, "with some babe who is there to amuse us outside the bounds of seriousness, we may pay attention to whether her mouth is small, her eyes blue, her bosom round enough . . . But where a woman's visage has other, higher messages to proclaim, she becomes beautiful through other, loftier forces." How true! The dreary realist politicians of amorous pleasure may anatomize the female. But the doglike pug nose of Miss R. bears the highest message of all: the unity of primal sensual lust. All other tidings proclaimed by a female countenance must renounce credibility. Deceptive unnaturalness is the final station on that sidetrack of sexuality which offers only reflectiveness, and for that very reason fails to arouse. More interesting is another type, which has not strayed so far from nature as the hysteric but nonetheless betrays a broken line. Here we see nothing of the great tragic vein of female troubles, just the sorrows of female trouble. Actresses always play from their sexuality. What airheads regard as the effect of "soul"—they feel it as soon as the speech gets softer—is the dramatic sublimation of meteruation. From this springs all the fashionable color of melancholy in sensitive moderns.

538 Like no other she brought into the consciousness of those with eyes to see the unity of the female and the actress, the harmony of their phases, the theatricality of a grace that has a face for every mood. She followed the fateful path of all primal but untimely powers.

539 An actress is a woman to the nth power, an actor the nth root of a man.

540 Male actors wear talent as a mask. The variability of a female visage is talent. Actresses who create masks are not women but actors.

541 If you let her play the most natural situation a woman can find herself in, you may discover an actress.

542 The art of the actress is sublimated sexuality. But away from the stage her fire has to be able to transform her steam back into bodily form.

543 Only a woman who expends all her energy in life retains enough for the stage. The comic walk-ons of life are bad actresses.

544 Crude treatment of actresses does not always make a director guilty of libel. Sometimes he commits a transfer of energy. Productive crudity forces to light the femininity of the actress, while the unproductive kind masculinizes her; the first awakens nature, the second only the sense of honor. With a Lulu who lacked sparkle, a director adopted the tone of a Jack the Ripper, and it worked.

545 Laughter at actors' vanity, at their addiction to applause and the like, is itself laughable. To play better, theater people need applause; even artificial applause suffices. The happy feeling so many actors display when they get applause from people they have paid to clap is proof of their artistry.

Scarcely anyone would have become a great actor if the public had been born without hands.

546 Personal interaction with poets is not always desirable. Above all I dislike the sleepwalkers who always fall onto the right side.

547 One will be forgiven for being lenient should those artists who do not work with words, the painters and musicians, display a certain degree of inability to rouse themselves mentally. But one must admit that artists mostly outdo art here, and are able to satisfy beyond the allowed measure the claims one makes on the silliness of entertainment. This is not true of the full personalities which burst with inspiration even outside art, even when they are silent—only of the average talented person, whose profession has left him nothing to spare for spiritual subsistence. When someone's spirituality dribbles away in tones or colors, there are times when you cannot keep him on the simplest train of thought. Which is not to say that poets can never be idiots. It was one of them, the sentimental type, who when someone once tried to explain an equation in two unknowns, looked at him and demonstrated the limits of his understanding with the assurance that for the moment the matter struck him as violet. A painter would not even be able to manage this much and would just leave his tongue hanging out. A musician would not do even that. In conversation with violin players I have withstood the torments of a martyr. One of them once congratulated me at the time of a great bank fraud. When I remarked that it was not my birthday, he opined that I had kept my reputation as a prophet. When I asked him what he was talking about, he referred to the fraud. I replied that I did not recall predicting it, but he had an answer for this: "Well—this whole state of affairs"—and fastened his full artist's gaze on me in gracious idiocy. This was a celebrated violinist. But people like this should not be allowed to roam about without a violin. Just as it should be forbidden, say, to

intervene in the private life of a singer. This experience can only be a disappointment, for both men and women. As soon as a singer opens his mouth to speak, or to reveal himself in some other way, things come to a bad end. The painter standing in the way of his canvas becomes a blotch, and after his work is done the musician is a false note. Whoever needs it should let tones and colors go to work on him, for heaven's sake. But it cannot be necessary to pile the potentialities of the unoccupied artistic soul onto the mass of stupidity already heaped high in the world.

548 Yes, the Grinzing Brook inspired Beethoven's Pastoral Symphony. But this proves nothing about the Grinzing Brook and everything about Beethoven. The smaller the landscape, the greater the work of art can be, and vice versa. But it is foolish to say that the mood a brook gives a random passerby is the same as the mood the listener gets from the resulting symphony. Otherwise you could also say the smell of rotten apples gives us Schiller's *Wallenstein*.

549 I certainly do not underestimate the value of scientific sexual research. Nonetheless it remains a beautiful assignment. And when its results are confirmed by the conclusions of artistic imagination, science is flattered and has not lived in vain.

550 On the pictures of those who create without a spiritual background and astonish the uninitiated with a certain verisimilitude, there ought to stand a notice: "copied from nature." If they were to draw a collection of wax figures, you could not tell the difference between the figures and the visitors.

551 The mark of a bad draughtsman is that once he has captured a figure with its mouth open it is impossible to imagine it ever closing again.

552 A soldier draughtsman, whose figures stand at attention for the observer.

553   When I see his illustrations, I think: the only thing God made in this world was a drum major!

554   Things never come to a stop so fast as when a bad draughtsman portrays motion. A good draughtsman can draw a runner with no legs.

555   The dancing girl of today can definitely dance Buddha. Only her uncle the ballet dancer is retarded in his development.

556   Modern taste needs the choicest complications to discover in the end that the cylinder is the most convenient form for a water glass. It achieves meaning on the path of inconveniences. It works in the sweat of its brow to recognize that the earth is not a cube but a ball. There is something stirring in the way civilization gapes like a savage at the achievements of nature.

557   An exclusive art form is a monster. It delivers art into the hands of the common crowd, because when only some of them can become insiders, they all want to, and art begins to live off the side effects of exclusivity.

558   We are cultured enough to avoid clubs that are merely "watering holes." But no cultured concertgoer is disturbed by the thought of letting himself be transported to the celestial spheres at the same time as five hundred other people. I have nothing against relieving myself in the company of my fellow citizens, but nothing could induce me to meet with a single one of them in the Isles of the Blessed.

559   The aesthete's life is not so far from the politician's as people think. Life resolves itself into a line for the politician, a surface for the aesthete. The void game they both play leads them equally far from the life of the mind, to some place where they are not even worth considering. It is tragic to be protested by one of these two when one wants nothing to do with the other, and to belong to one group just because one despises the other. But from the heights of true spiritu-

ality one comes to see politics as just an aesthetic bauble and the orchid as a partisan flower. The same lack of personality drives one to reduce life to matter, the other to form. They want nothing to do with each other, but they belong at the same slaughterhouse.

560 The politician is plugged in to life, one knows not where. The aesthete flees life, one knows not whither.

561 Not to seek reality and not to flee it, but to create it, and create it all the more by destroying it: how is this blessing supposed to enter brains through whose windings the muck of the world is swept twice a day? The public feels itself superior to nothing so much as an author whom it does not understand; but military types who never could, never did prove themselves behind a shop counter—these are its heroes. It took a God to endure what the journalists say.

Six

562   There are two sorts of writers. Those who are, and those who aren't. With the first, content and form belong together, like soul and body; with the second, they merely match, like body and clothes.

563   The written word ought to be the embodiment of a thought, a physical necessity, not the socially acceptable husk of an opinion.

564   If you generate opinions you cannot let yourself be caught in contradictions. If you have thoughts you think between the contradictions too.

565   Views reproduce by division, thoughts by budding.

566   An idea is far better served when given a form unsuitable for the direct route to the masses. If it travels that way only via the dam of a personality, it goes further than if it popularizes itself. The real test of its load capacity is the artwork it

spawns, rather than the immediate effect it achieves between the slick covers of a trendy tract. Either an idea serves an artwork or the work serves the idea. If the idea streams across into art, it evaporates into deep space and is not initially perceived on earth. In the other case it floods its way out of the tract to the river mouth of the contemporary brain. But an idea should be able to say of itself that it seldom goes into society.

567 The true agitators for a cause are those who are more serious about form. Art blocks the immediate effect in favor of a higher. So its products are not blockbusters. They would not set sales records even if the hawkers were to tout "sensational revelations from the secret trove of the German vocabulary!"

568 Thought is a love child. Opinion is recognized in bourgeois society.

569 What enters the ear easily leaves easily too. What goes in hard comes out hard. This goes for writing even more than music making.

570 Not forgiving the manner means not forgiving the matter.

571 Sexual issues should not be discussed on street corners. Experience them, formulate them, but do not talk about them. Hypocrisy in defense of truth is no vice.

572 An author who immortalizes a routine case compromises only the ephemeral present. But one who journalizes eternity can expect recognition in the best society.

573 Why does no one demand that a musician write a symphony protesting social abuses? It is ages since I made any incidental music.

574 You do not become an author just by using the language to call a cabinet minister unfit for office.

575   The material the musician molds is tones; the painter speaks
       in colors. So no honorable layman who speaks only in words
       presumes to judge music and painting. The writer shapes
       raw material accessible to everyone: the written word. So
       every reader presumes to judge verbal art. The illiterates of
       tone and color are modest. But people who can read pass
       for more than illiterates.

576   Language is the raw material of the literary artist; but it does
       not belong to him alone, while color does belong exclusive-
       ly to the painter. Ordinary people should be forbidden to
       speak. Sign language is perfectly sufficient for the sort of
       thoughts they have to share. Are we allowed incessantly to
       smear our clothes with oils?

577   Is writing nothing more than the skill of verbally imparting
       an opinion to the public? That would make painting the art
       of voicing an opinion in colors. But the journalists of paint-
       ing are called—house painters. And I believe that a writer is
       the man who speaks an artwork to the public. It was the
       highest honor ever accorded me when a reader confessed
       with some embarrassment that he could only understand my
       things on the second reading. He hesitated to say it to me;
       he was reticent about expressing my opinion. This man was
       a connoisseur and did not know it. Praise of my style leaves
       me cold, but the reproaches against it are about to make me
       arrogant. I spent a long time afraid people would take plea-
       sure in my writings on first reading.—What? Are good
       phrases to serve as nothing more than mouthwash for the
       public?—The Sunday magazine writers who write in Ger-
       man have an immense head start on the verbal artists who
       write from German. They beguile on the first glance and
       disappoint on the second; as if one were standing behind the
       scenes and suddenly saw it is all made of cardboard. With
       the others the first reading is as if the stage were veiled. Who
       is going to applaud that? The hacks hiss before the curtain
       even goes up. Most people do. They have no time. Only for

works of linguistic art do they have no time. With paintings they are prepared to concede that you should not just portray the first impression of an event; they wring from themselves a second look, so they can also feel something of the color artistry. But—an art of sentence construction? If you tell them such a thing exists, they think you are talking about good grammar.

578   In linguistics an author does not have to be infallible. Even the use of impure materials can advance an artistic agenda. I do not avoid provincialisms when they serve a satiric purpose. When wit presupposes received ideas and familiar jargon, it prefers common speech to correct speech, and nothing is further from its mind than purist ambitions. It is about verbal art. Only five people in a thousand even sense such a thing exists. The others see an opinion, and hanging on it, a joke you can conveniently slip into your buttonhole. They have no clue about the secret of organic growth. They value only the raw material. You may transform the most vulgar notion into the most profound effect, but under the eye of such people it will become vulgar again. Triviality as an element of satiric form: all that remains in their hand is a stale pun.

579   Wordplay, contemptible as an end in itself, can become the noblest medium of artistic purposes when it serves to abbreviate a witty view. It can be a sociological epigram.

580   In wit linguistic triviality is often the content of artistic expression. The writer who uses it is capable of genuine solemnity. Pathos in and of itself is just as worthless as pure triviality.

581   The form is the thought. It makes mediocre seriousness into deeper wit. For instance, if I say that in a children's room where wild young scamps are playing the mother's heart should be unbreakable.

582 It is impossible to imitate or plagiarize an author whose art is the word. One would have to go to the trouble of transcribing his entire oeuvre. Words can be taken away if they stand in themselves, imprint themselves on the memory of the average person and thus have no great value. How shallow and empty they seem in the new surroundings. Unrecognizable! A joke born naturally as the inevitable expression of anger sometimes has the misfortune of sitting so loosely that any lout who passes by can rip it off. The blossom lets itself be plucked but withers rapidly, whether a reader puts it in his hat band or a literary hack in his leafless tree. In a way these are the blossoms requiring particularly jealous guarding, as they are the only ones the public knows about. I have touched on some nasty subjects and made a few good jokes about them. Quite a few people know this. But they cannot quote the better ones. If the author succeeds in fitting together at one stroke far-flung backgrounds, objects, signs of the times, so that one thought becomes an abbreviated essay; if even wordplay can evoke pathos; then there is no chance of folksiness.

583 You have to read my works twice to get close to them. But I have nothing against it if people read them three times. Still, rather than read them just once I prefer they not read them at all. I do not want to be responsible for causing congestion in a flathead who has no time.

584 You have to read all writers twice. The good ones you remember, the bad ones you dismember.

585 He is a master of his native language—this is a military man. The artist is a servant to the word.

586 There are writers who can express in a mere twenty pages things I sometimes need two whole lines for.

587 The intellectual total of a literary piece should be the result of multiplication, not addition.

588 The writer's development: In the beginning you are used to it and it is a piece of cake. But then it gets more and more difficult, and when you are really practiced there are some sentences you cannot even finish.

589 A book can deceive you as to whether it offers the author's worldview or one he is just presenting. A sentence is the test of whether it has one at all.

590 You cannot dictate an aphorism into a machine. It would take too long.

591 Once I saw during the editing of my writings for the book edition that somewhere I had expressed the conflict between natural drives and sexual ethics in the single sentence: "Thus the children of this era grow up knowing nothing about what they must and so much about what they must not do." The typesetter, anticipating the standpoint of the intelligent reader, had changed the sentence thus: "Thus the children of this era grow up knowing nothing about what they must know and so much about what they must not do." A quite comprehensible opinion, which will give no reader a head-ache: it touches on the problem of sex education. And it is much more obliging than the other view, which also has the disadvantage of being open to destruction by a single typo.

592 An aphorism does not need to be true, but it should out-wing the truth. It must get beyond it with a spin.

593 A journalist is someone who takes what the reader has al-ready thought anyway and expresses it in a form not just any military man could manage.

594 Is it permitted to take a footbath in the wellspring of the language? If so they should forbid drinking from it.

595 The highest compliment one can pay the literati of today is that they keep the magazines on life-support. But how does

it sound when one tells them they are keeping life on magazine-support?

596 Sunday magazine writers and hairdressers are equally involved with people's heads.

597 To write for a Sunday magazine is to curl locks on a bald head.

598 The most dangerous literati are whose good memory absolves them of all responsibility. They say they can do nothing for it, nothing against it if something flies into their heads. Somehow I prefer an honest plagiarist.

599 First the dog sniffs about, then he lifts his leg. One cannot reasonably object to this lack of originality. But hoping the literary hack will read before he writes is a lost cause.

600 One man writes because he sees, the other because he hears.

601 In literature there are two different kinds of similarity: when you find that one author is related to another, and when you discover they are merely acquaintances.

602 For his education a writer should live more than read. For his entertainment he should write more than read. This makes for books that can both educate and entertain the public.

603 I know no more difficult reading than light reading. The imagination bumps up against graphic descriptions and tires too quickly to work any further on its own steam. One flies through the lines that describe a garden wall, and the mind lingers on an ocean. How pleasurable the voluntary journey would be, if the rudderless ship did not choose just the wrong moment to smash back into the garden wall. Difficult reading offers dangers one can survey in advance. It harnesses one's forces, while easy reading sets them loose and leaves them to their own devices. Difficult reading can be a danger for weak powers. Lighter reading is the danger for stronger

powers. The mind has to be a worthy match for the difficult; the easy is no match for the mind.

604   In literary work I find enjoyment, but literary enjoyment is turning into work. To enjoy the product of another mind I must first take a critical stance, i.e., transform my reading into work. This is why writing a book remains so much more agreeable and easy for me than reading one.

605   The truly, relentlessly productive mind does not easily adjust to reading. It relates to a reader as a locomotive relates to a pleasure traveler. You would not ask a tree how it likes the landscape.

606   Writing a novel may be a pure pleasure. Living a novel— here you start getting into difficulties. But reading a novel I avoid as far as humanly possible.

607   Where do I find the time to not read so much?

608   The reader is happy to let an author put his education to shame. He is impressed that he did not know what Corfu is called in Albanian; from now on he will know and can one-up people who still do not. Education is the only premise the public does not resent, and the author who humbles the reader with it can be sure of being man of the hour. But woe to him who requires abilities that are hard to catch up with or strenuous to exercise! It is fine for the author to know more than the reader, but for him to have thought more is not so easily forgiven. The public is not allowed to be stupid-er. Indeed it is cleverer than the cultivated author, since it learned right from its magazine what Corfu is called in Alba-nian, while the author had to go look it up in a lexicon.

609   Reading one of his mythological-political treatises, you learn to hate culture more than is absolutely necessary.

610   The deeply felt lack of personality created a kind of mental fire alarm. Oxen run out of their stall into the fire; the pun-

dit runs from his material into culture. Amidst the mental fumes you hold your nose.

611 An agitator seizes the stage. A dramatist is seized by the stage.

612 Acquiring personality within a party is certainly inconceivable. But even when one stands outside the parties one cannot always evade the necessity of acknowledging a color that turns out to be a party color. This is fatal, but as a writer one has an honorable way out: tone of voice. To the masses the opinion may be the main thing; one must differentiate oneself from them by the tone in which one utters it. A journalist who has courted the aristocratic viewpoint for years feels shortchanged in a legal battle with an aristocrat and discovers: "It makes no difference whether the plaintiff is called Moltke or Cohen, for all citizens are equal in the eyes of the law and the courts." This is merely true, which is bad. It is true, but it is said in brute earnest, as if this claim were the culmination of the speaker's entire intellectual life. In a similar situation I would make the same claim, but I believe that no matter how emphatic I was there would still be a chasm between me and my allies: the court would realize its unfairness, but democracy would demand suspension of equal rights in my favor. When I have to make a liberal demand, I do it in such a way that reactionaries parry it and progressives disown me. It comes down to the tone of voice, the detachment in one's speech. Saying everything in the same tone with the same detachment is a sign of meager literary gifts.

613 The diplomat E. was accused of sexual relations with a man named Earnest, and the journalist H. writes the following about E's diplomatic abilities: "Too often this ass has failed to take an earnest stand." If Heine had written this sentence, he would have quickly added: naturally not in every sense of the words. It would have been a petty point, in the style of those low blows against Platen which for some

strange reason failed to smother their author's reputation. Heine would have made the joke, or at least immediately remarked that the seriously intended sentence was a joke—either way, low marks for creativity. But the other H. lacks the ability to tell a joke or even to sense the humorous implications. Now there is nothing more exquisitely embarrassing for an able writer than the possibility of producing unintended notions in the reader. Better not to express what you mean than to express what you do not mean. The author has to know all the paths of thought his words could open up. He has to know what will happen to his words. The more relationships they evoke, the greater the artistry; but they must not enter relations hidden from the artist. Someone who relates the diplomat E. to "taking an earnest stand" without noticing he has created a joke is no author. But stressing the humorous reading does not exactly inspire my respect either. I would have suppressed the serious remark, because its humor would have bumped into me, and if I had thought of the crack, I would not have written it.

614 A jackass thinks my verdict on H's style—"turgidity is a crutch"—is a confession of my own faults. Certainly I am sometimes as "hard to comprehend" as H. We are at the same distance from the coffeehouse readers. It is just that H. impatiently rushes on ahead of them, leaving all of political mythology in the lurch, still far from finished with his subzero thought; while I succeed in running away from them. It is the difference between fat and muscle. The reader may like the taste of fat better, but it is sad that he confuses two such different corporealities. Otherwise I am happy to allow that there are authors who get the better of me through their flaw of easy comprehensibility. This distinction too only a few are in a position to grasp: between a style that makes thought into language and language into thought, and a style where language is merely the husk of an opinion.

Today it is possible to confuse a sculptor with a tailor, because both produce forms.

615 Chronic neologism is a symptom of linguistic cancer.

616 Using unusual words is bad literary manners. The only difficulties one is allowed to lay in the public's way are conceptual.

617 The rats leave the sinking ship after they have got indigestion eating the blubber. This sums up the retinue and the style of a certain German publicist.

618 Heine is a Moses who struck his staff against the cliff of the German language. But speed is no magic; the water did not flow from the cliff; he had brought it there with his other hand, and it was eau de cologne.

619 Heine created the highest that can be created with the language. What can be created from the language stands higher.

620 One of the most insignificant, most famous of Heinrich Heine's poems begins with the question of what the lonesome teardrop wants, the one that is clouding the poet's vision. As he himself admits, it has remained in his eye for many a long year, but in spite of this it is conserved in an undried state all the way through the poem. Although it is he who has robbed himself of the possibility of a clear view, this lyricist has for once succeeded in sculpting tears. I almost want to credit him with discovering the poetry of the ocular sty.

621 Where there is no strength for either crying or laughing, humor smiles beneath tears.

622 Sentimental irony is a dog that barks at the moon as he pisses on graves.

623 I know a species of sentimental scribbler that is dull and stinks. Mosquitoes from Heine's mattress-grave.

624 In literature one must watch out for sentence structure swindlers. Their houses have windows before they have walls.

625 Mental confectioners deliver candied reading fruit.

626 "Writing well" without personality can be enough for journalism. For science in any case. But never for literature.

627 So many people write because they lack the character not to.

628 Wittiness is sometimes witlessness bubbling without restraint.

629 Saphir's popularity knew no bounds. He never cluttered the public's path with thoughts or disturbed it with convictions. His inspirations were stumbled upon, his poetry was chatter.

630 German literati: the laurels one dreams about keep another awake. Another dreams that his laurels are giving insomnia to yet another, and that one cannot sleep because the other is dreaming of laurels.

631 Recently, as I was introduced to one of our young poets, the question slipped out of me: "So which bank do you write for?" This was quite unpremeditated; I had no intention of insulting the poor devil.

632 Sunday magazine writers are frustrated haberdashers. Their parents force them into an intelligent profession, but the original talent forces its way out.

633 There are shallow and deep airheads.

634 The idea of a journalist writing just as correctly about a new opera as about a new parliamentary rule of order is somewhat oppressive. Doubtless he could also instruct a bacteriologist, an astronomer, perhaps even a priest. And if an ex-

pert in higher mathematics crossed his path, he would prove to him that he is at home in even higher mathematics.

635   A hack writer's wit is at best the summer lightning of a mentality, somewhere in the distance. The only thought that strikes home is the one with the thunder of pathos right on its heels.

636   Journalism thinks without the pleasure of thought. The artist banished to such precincts resembles a hetaera forced into prostitution. Except that she succumbs without injury even here. Compulsory pleasure can mean diversion for her, but only aversion for him.

637   Prostitutes and journalists share the ability to numb themselves. Prostitutes have the added ability not to numb themselves.

638   The public will not swallow everything. It rejects immoral writing with outrage as soon as it notices its cultural intent.

639   Something need not necessarily suffer in the eyes of the public just because it is artistic. One overestimates the public if one believes it takes offense at an excellent presentation. It pays no attention at all to the quality of the presentation and placidly accepts valuable work, so long as its object accidentally corresponds to some vulgar interest.

640   A good writer does not get nearly as many anonymous poison-pen letters as is customarily assumed. Out of a hundred jackasses there are scarcely ten who will admit their nature, and one at most who will put it in writing.

641   A journal is not well run unless the critical scribblings of the fans are guided by an act of the editor's will. A reader's disillusion should not plunge an author into confusion. If he cannot win it over to his view of life, he is better off being ruined materially by its outrage than mentally by his capitulation.

642 The world silently tosses journalism the finest works as plunder, and the fearsome question remains open, whether the trade has not already destroyed the literary sensibility of future ages too.

643 The flatheads are victorious across the board. This realization closes one in like a wall, behind which the one remaining privilege is despair. But the wall does not stay still, it draws ever closer. It is Poe's vision of the pit and the pendulum. "Down—steadily down it crept. I took a frenzied pleasure in contrasting its downward with its lateral velocity. To the right—to the left—far and wide. . . . I alternately laughed and howled, as the one or the other idea grew predominant. Down—certainly, relentlessly down! It vibrated within three inches of my bosom!" A friend consoles me with the thought that the comparison holds only in part, since the fountain at whose brim the prisoner stands signifies not a torture device but the creative possibility of mastering all this terror.

644 Lichtenberg digs deeper than any other, but he does not surface afterward. He speaks underground. Only people who dig equally deep can hear him.

645 It does no injury to one's admiration for Schopenhauer if one occasionally feels the truths of his minor essays are noise. He complains about doors slamming, and how vividly he complains! You practically hear the doors being slammed—the open doors.

646 It is rare for old books to retain a living content between the arcane and the mundane.

647 In the beginning was the review copy. A reviewer received one in the mail from the publisher. He wrote a review. Then he wrote a book. The publisher accepted it and circulated review copies. The next reviewer who received one did as the first. This is how modern literature was born.

648   The young Jean Paul resolved "to write books so he could buy books." Our young writers have resolved to get books for free so they can write books.

649   Schiller sat rotten apples on his desk for dramatic inspiration. Since then German audiences are afraid to employ them as a deterrent.

650   Like murderers in Shakespeare, literary men are now lining up to murder Shakespeare. They too are comic figures and their task too is thankless. Only their capability is lesser, and in the end they lie stretched out like murder victims in Shakespeare.

651   Correctors of Schlegel's Shakespeare translations! Breaking the wings a word has sprouted—this only a philological conscience can do.

652   A houseboy in Nestroy deals with the burden of life, tossing boredom out on its ear. He has a sturdier grip than a professor of philosophy.

653   Someone should start a mental elevator service to spare us the outrageous exertions involved in descending to the *niveau* of today's writing. By the time I climb back up to myself I am always quite out of breath.

654   My good ear allows me to imitate an actor I saw only once, decades ago, playing a servant in a provincial theater. This is a real curse. Anyone I have heard once I hear forever. The only people I never hear are the contemporary writers whose Sunday magazine pieces I read. So I have to appoint each one a special role. When I read a Viennese newspaper article, I hear a headwaiter, or a peddler who sold me a bill of goods once years ago. Or a lecture from my cleaning lady. In short, I have to switch into some mental dialect to get through it. But it is doubtless the author's voice.

655 With many writers the work is collateral for the personality. With others the work is collaterally damaged by the personality. Whether you want to or not, you have to think of him while reading, in every ironic shrug of the shoulders, every indifferent wave of the hand.

656 The dramatist should balance the scales between the stage and the audience. When his characters sit down for conversation, the audience fidgets as if it wanted to stand up. Only motion onstage ensures quiet in the audience. Sitting down onstage is the cue for boredom offstage.

657 My glance fell on the last page of the drama *Youth*. How young literature was back then! Little Hans throws himself over little Ann's corpse with the call "de—ad!" If it were just "dead," I suppose the actor would have missed the mark. In fact, naturalism was the swimming instructor of inadequacy. When it was not providing the water wings of dialect it at least held out such stage instructions as a lifeguard's pole.

658 Nature has a truth higher than the little reality German literature has trotted out for two decades in the sweat of its brow, to deliver meager proofs of its existence.

659 The narrowness of a petty artist first becomes disturbing when he becomes conscious of it and turns toward the outside world. With P's portrayals of Vienna, though they are full of lyrical prose, I feel as if a one-horse carriage had awakened the Hippocrene. With his critical pieces I notice that the wellspring of his muse is in Boethia.

660 A pornographic writer can easily have talent. The broader the bounds of the terminology, the slighter the psychological exertion. When I am permitted to use lowest-common-denominator terms for the sexual act, the game is half won. The effect of a forbidden word counterbalances all tension

and the contrast between the surprising and the familiar is almost an element of humor.

661 Just as there are always new faces, although the human content varies little, so there must always be new sentences despite similar mental material. Here as elsewhere it comes down to the creator who has the ability to express the gentlest nuance.

662 A creative head has its own way of saying even what another has said before. Because of this another person can imitate thoughts which have not yet entered the creative head.

663 Private thoughts need not always be new. But someone with a new thought can easily have got it from someone else.

664 A new insight must be expressed in a way that makes it seem merely accidental that the sparrows on the roof neglected to whistle it out.

665 There are truths that prove their discoverers witless.

666 Political journalism: what matters is not the size of the target but the distance.

667 It sometimes takes more courage and liveliness to attack a carter than a king.

668 You can write a whole book about a nobody who would be overly honored with a single line.

669 Putting satirical constructions on events, however little they may mean objectively, gives me a pleasure that has never been taken away by the fear of making the victims known or beloved. I have always shown the smallest offense too much honor.

670 An artless truth about an evil is an evil. It must be worthy in itself. Then it reconciles itself with the evil, and with pain about the existence of evils.

671 Abusive language cannot be condemned as such. Only when it stands by itself and for itself. A stylist must be able to use an abusive term as if no taxi-driver had ever used it before. Incompetence seeks out unaccustomed words, but a master says even the most commonplace thing for the first time. His threat to box someone's ears can be not only the organic expression of a mood but also a thought. *Götz von Berlichingen* can be a new release.

672 One should not always name names. What should be said is not that someone did it but that it was possible.

673 A pathetic derision, which rants itself out in punctuation, using question marks and dashes as whips, nets and spears.

674 If you have wit you can make old jokes too. They are never borrowed: people believe them transformed. Even when a child resembles a stranger to a T, it is still one's own. More important than the child is its birth.

675 Retailing a witticism means simply: picking up an arrow. How it was shot the quote does not say.

676 It is often difficult to write an aphorism when you can. It is much easier to write an aphorism when you can't.

677 Reproaching a writer with vanity is beside the point. When he writes that he considers himself a significant author, he may be able to prove it with that very sentence, while a musician even attempting incidental music on this theme would make himself a liar.

678 Secrets kept from individuals do not have to be secrets kept from the public. They are in better hands with the public, because there you determine the form of the information yourself. The man who sees the form as the true content reserves rights to every word. He can confidently face charges of secretiveness, or extreme shamelessness, or both.

679 I am always prepared to publish what I have told a friend under the seal of deepest discretion. But he must never pass it on.

680 To be tired of life because one has found a flaw in one's work which no one else sees; to calm down only when you find a second flaw, since then the stain on your honor is covered beneath the knowledge of human imperfection: it seems to me it is this kind of talent for self-torture that distinguishes art from handicraft. Shallow thinkers may consider this trait pedantic; but they have no idea of the freedom that gives birth to such compulsion, or what ease of production such self-burdening leads to. Nothing could be more foolish than speaking of formalistic fussiness in a case where form is not the clothing of a thought but its substance. This hunt for the final possibilities of expression leads into the guts of language. Here is created that interwovenness where the border of What and How is no longer determinable, so that often the expression preceded the thought, until it gave off a spark under the rubbing of the file. Dilettantes work surely and live contentedly. I have often stopped the press and destroyed a print run just because the milligram scales of my stylistic sense rejected a word. Machines rape the mind instead of serving it; the mind wants to show them who is boss. But publication cannot be delayed indefinitely, nor does it bring the caesura I have longed for in my creative labors. So when am I actually finished?—I am not finished with one work until I go on to another. That is how long my "authorial correction" lasts, together with the life-giving folly of believing that the reader will notice the absence of an insight born after the fact. And even writing that so bloodily regrets its imperfection cannot trouble the complacency of this reader, his reading ability degenerated through journalism. For a few groschen he has acquired the right to superficiality; would he cover his costs, if he had to enter into the work? It would perhaps be more fitting for German authors to apply to their

manuscripts even one-tenth of the care I devote after the fact to my print runs. A friend, who often accompanied me as midwife, was astonished how easy my births were and how heavy my childbed. Things go well for the others. They work at their desks and enjoy themselves in society. I enjoy myself at the desk and work in society. So I avoid society. At best I can ask people whether they like this or that word better. And that they do not know.

681   A good author will always fear the public noticing which thoughts occurred to him too late. But here the public is more indulgent than one might think, and does not notice the thoughts he did have either.

682   One must write each time as if one wrote for the first and last time, say as much as if it were a farewell and say it as well as if one were going through one's debut.

683   I am not the master of language; but language masters me completely. She is not the servant of my thoughts. I have a liaison with her: I receive thoughts, and she can do with me what she wishes. I parry her word for word, for from the word the young thought springs toward me and retroactively forms the language that created it. Such divine grace of intellectual pregnancy forces one to one's knees and makes every expense of trembling care a duty. Thought is servant and language is mistress; if someone knows how to invert the relationship she makes herself useful in his house but forbids him her privates.

684   From close by the oldest word should seem unfamiliar, newly born and awakening doubt whether it is alive. Then it really is alive. You hear the heart of language beating.

685   O joy of linguistic experiences, thrilling to the bone! The danger of the word is the pleasure of the thought. What turned there at the corner? Not yet seen and already beloved! I throw myself into this adventure.

Seven

686 I set my quill on the Austrian corpse, because I still believe the corpse breathes life.

687 Prussia: Freedom of movement, with a muzzle. Austria: Solitary confinement, with permission to scream.

688 I know a bureaucracy that is more interested in income than insight.

689 The Austrian nationalities unite to swear allegiance at court, and quarrel over precedence in courting royal favor.

690 In Germany it only takes two people to make an interest group. If one dies, the other gives himself a promotion as a sign of grief.

691 In the pouring rain I saw a sprinkler truck going through the streets. Why the sprinkler when it is already raining, I asked. Because the dirt sweeper is in front of the truck, was the answer.

692 The police watch keenly to make sure only the aged and ugly surrender themselves to vice. In a bordello a woman is arrested only if her depravity dates from an earlier police era, if her virtue pretty much fell with the Linien Walls. She has to be an emeritrix . . . The women too old for the trade sing: Them walls held us up!

693 Oh, the coarsely businesslike Berlin prostitutes! For his two marks the Viennese is accustomed to demanding spiritual devotion and the feeling of sole possession.

694 A city where the men say erstwhile virgins have "given it up" deserves to be razed.

695 You feel yourself driven by a demonic power; these people bawl at you that "mainstream values" are their whole life, which you thereupon want to take away from them.

696 Tuning in to the Viennese temperament: the eternal tuning of an unequal-tempered orchestra.

697 The kitchen: vegetables and brains prepared with flour.

698 To prevent confusion, the Viennese distinguishes between "eats" and "it's."

699 You sometimes read that a city has so-and-so hundred thousand "souls," but it sounds exaggerated. For the same reason it is time to break with the system of census by "heads." One would stop being mistrustful of the seven-figure statistics if a more common body part were used as the census unit. No one could go on saying such an estimate—for example in the case of a metropolis like Vienna—was exaggerated. The intake and output of food are unquestionably the most important interests determining the spiritual life of a people. The only sad thing is that they have so little control even over what is most important to them. The culture of this activity is definitely not advancing; it may confer distinc-

tion to be a strong eater, but not to be a loud one, making comfort sounds that can be heard all the way overseas.

700 Where have I seen that face? You think and think and the answer will not come. Maybe it really is someone you are meeting for the first time? Finally you have it. What kind of person is he? Why, he produces shoes, or his clocks are the best, or—don't buy hats from anyone else! Yes, even his face, smiling down to us from billboards, as if it were showing us a restaurant bill from its conciliatory side; this face, greeting us from a meadow along our train route—this face alone is sufficient recommendation of his wares. What a goodly watchmaker he must be, what a charming hatmaker, an enchanting shoemaker! And towering above them all, the rubber king! Who could resist him? Who could contemplate these reliable features for an instant without being seduced into sampling the unbreakable bond of human trust? This face, where heartiness and cleverness mate, is almost love itself—the love that makes caution sole mother of wisdom. It turns into the face of the voyeur, following us into secret places. And we do need to ask ourselves sometimes whether we have to put up with that. Whether in fact we should sense in this face one of those exceptional inhibitions the erotic sense cannot cope with. We might want to ask whether the happiness promised by these eyes could not be enjoyed without these eyes, whether we can conceive of a honeymoon unchaperoned by the rubber king. But there is no Good Taste Police to spare us from constantly associating the wares with the well-known dealer, and so the dance row of prominent personalities winds its way through the life of a Vienna day. On top of all this there is the flurry of physiognomies—this one enraptured, that one disgusted—assuring us every day in the advertising columns how desolate life is without Kleider Barley Malt Liquor, and how perfect it is once you have discovered it. You could say this Viennese existence is not without its variety of strong impressions.

701   The most popular faces in Vienna are the two Heurigen proprietors. They are billboarded on every street corner, larger than life, and their fame certainly has the greatness of survival. In rather the same way the Germans impressed on their minds the forms of Goethe and Schiller. But the Austrian cultural *niveau* is definitely higher. With Goethe and Schiller the Germans have only the decorative relationship produced by the sham of education, while there is definitely an inner connection between the Viennese and their heroes. One day grandfathers will tell attentive grandchildren that they saw Wolf in Gersthof, and grandmothers will be rejuvenated by the memory of Hartwieger's eye resting on them.

702   The way things stand today, if Goethe returned he would surely be deported for Unauthorized Reversification.

703   I have observed in the Italians not only that they are devoted to bel canto in every phase of life but also that their serious side is serious operetta. If, in the theater, the stanzas of the chin-chin-chinaman make them call out "bis" until the singer's throat bursts, there is no great harm done. But their life too flows away like the plot of *Geisha:* a production designed for Saxon audiences to comprehend and enjoy. In feminine psychology I do not believe the Italians have transcended the realization: *la donna e mobile.* If someone dared to question it, someone else would assuredly respond: *eppur si muove!*

704   The sense of the phrase "strain at a gnat and swallow a camel" has never been as clear to me as here in Italy, where loving hosts spread a mosquito net over our beds.

705   Hamburg beds have a high rim. You are certain you will not fall out in a stormy sea. A custom grown nonsensical, through which the natives preserve the tradition of the shipboard berth. Seasickness propagates itself onshore via generations of carpenters, and nothing is more painful upon arising than the remembrance that Hamburgers are a seafaring people.

706   With German coffee I noticed an exaggerated compliancy toward milk. It pales as soon as milk comes anywhere near. This could also serve as a picture of relations between the sexes in this country.

707   On Scandinavian trains it is "Ikke lene sik ud"; in Germany, "Do not lean out!" In Austria, "It is forbidden to lean out the window." Outside this country they say: it's your own fault if you do it, or: you have yourself to blame for the consequences. To idiots here at home we say: it is forbidden to do away with yourself. For fear of punishment quite a few will abstain from killing themselves.—A broadminded social spirit forbids what encroaches on other people's rights. A mistaken individualism says: if there is something you do not want to happen to you, don't do it to yourself. I will not be persuaded the prohibition against smoking in Austrian railway coupes is anything but a warning against nicotine poisoning.

708   There are three levels of civilization. The first: when respectable restaurants do not post rules of etiquette. The second: when they post rules directing guests to put their clothes in order before leaving the establishment. The third: when the directions are followed by the justification that propriety demands them. This highest level of civilization is the one we stand on.

709   The madding crowd: after the accident happened "many curious people showed up to inspect the scene of the accident." But the accident was already so dulled to the provocations of the curious that it contented itself with silent contempt.

710   On a winter Sunday afternoon in a Viennese coffeehouse, cooped up between card-playing fathers, shrieking women and children reading comics, one can be seized by such a strong feeling of loneliness that one longs for whatever bustling life there might presently be in the Advent Bay.

Countries and People   101

711   In this city there are people and institutions, coachmen, pubs and the like, whose popularity seems incomprehensible. But a little reflection brings one to the conclusion that they are popular because they are in demand.

712   The people who serve us are sights to behold. The coachman is a personality, so I cannot go anywhere. The waiter is a person of quality, so he lets me wait for my food. The coal man sings happily on his coach, and I freeze.

713   In the emotional life of coachmen and town porters what I prize most is gratitude. Their souls have a kind of taxi stand. If I go by it, someone whose services I used once, ten years ago, will still wish me good day. If I am lucky enough to live next to it, I must hear and return such wishes several times a day. If the coachmen are at their coaches, then as often as I pass they point to their coaches and explain to me that they are coaches. This always happens when I do not need a ride. If I do need a ride, nothing happens because there is no driver. But then they will not tolerate my flagging down a passing hackney carriage either. If I get ready to do that they all come bolting out of the pub across from the abandoned depot and express their outrage in unforgettable terms. If I do meet one of them at his coach and want to climb in, he addresses me imperiously with the exclamation "Ahm occyepahd!" If by some chance he is not occyepahd, then some barefoot man barges in, opens the coach door for me and starts washing the coach. The coachman knows I am in a hurry, so he uses the cleaning time to drink coffee and take leave of his colleagues. Who knows where the journey will lead or what one will encounter. But then he climbs onto the coachbox, and after he has uncovered the horse and the meter, if there is one—then it gets serious.

714   Egypt would not be that far. But getting to the South Station!

715 Here in Austria there are unpunctual trains that cannot get the hang of their scheduled delays.

716 We humans must rely ever more on the machine, and in Vienna even the machine does not work. It does not go. Nothing goes, everything slows to a standstill. If a new restaurant opens, you would think it was the first restaurant ever. Everything slows, full of expectation. But the restaurant doesn't make a go of it. Nothing goes here, and nobody. I have never yet seen a Berliner stand still. Otherwise his physical mass would turn out to be slighter than that of the Viennese—who in turn must never go fast, or he would fall over. Everything stands still and waits: waiters, coaches, governments. Everything waits for the end—"a happy end of the world to you, your Grace!"—and even demands a tip for it. Our lifelong cry: we can wait. When a government minister falls, we can wait. When a horse falls, we can wait. We stand and stare up at the roof because someone else does. The steaming hot coffee stands at our table; the restaurateur, the director, the executive all stand to greet us, at our service. A royal equipage causes a traffic jam. We can wait. The Berliner goes. The Viennese slows to a standstill, in all situations. He doesn't even go under. A coachman has to bring forth the shouts of a Homeric hero to warn a pedestrian; and one notices when people finally have to go that they have not learned to do so. But as I said, they do stand superbly. Go—they can only go behind an archduke, amid music from the Burg. Vienna is full of such "marks of distinction" and every Viennese feels he is one of them: the youngest Billy-Bob likes to see himself as "standin' tall." That could be very beautiful, very proud, self-legitimizing. If it were a Goethe that stood tall. But when an imbecile blocks the way, a Goethe cannot move forward.

717 Social life is possible here in Vienna only on the condition that everyone restrict the act of thought to his private quar-

ters. One must count one's blessings that the right to physical existence is at least theoretically recognized, though it is endangered every hour by unregulated city traffic. A smooth resolution of life's external necessities would permit one to come to one's senses. In a city where the coachmen have to bellow "Huh!" and "Hah!", where every pedestrian gapes at every vehicle and every vehicle at every pedestrian, it is a personal accomplishment to get home with limbs intact. The swarming of Friedrich Street in Berlin disturbs my thoughts less than the well-known quiet alleys of the Vienna suburbs, beloved of literary men from nonpatrician families. When the mill is making noise, the miller can sleep soundly. And his dream is more beautiful than the poetry of our reality.

718 Every Viennese is a public monument, every Berliner a public conveyance.

719 If I were to ask the porter of a Berlin restaurant what the bas-reliefs and friezes in the stairwell mean, he might answer: "That is to give the sense of beauty its due." If I ask the rag-and-bone man there who a monument represents, he might answer: "He done helped the schools." Certainly these are horrors of civilization. But one warms to their advantages with time, when the only answer such questions ever get in Vienna is: "You revolting little pig, who's going to give you a second look!"

720 Vienna and Berlin. I need automobiles, to come to my senses faster. The Ambraser collection I have within myself. Maybe the Capucin Crypt.

721 To me the smooth resolution of life's external necessities is a deeper cultural problem than the protection of the Karls-kirche. I am confident that such churches can only come into being when we preserve intact all our inner possessions, all intellectual rights and all productive energies of the nervous system—not let them be consumed by the resistance of the political machines.

722 The streets of Vienna are paved with culture. Other cities' with asphalt.

723 When in a Vienna restaurant six "meal bearers" ask me whether I have "already ordered" and not one takes my order; when the cry "check, please!" propagates like an echo without being heard; when the division of tips according to seniority, merit and position pushes out all other problems that might be going through my head—for all this the beauty of the Burgplatz outside can offer only slight compensation.

724 The biggest curse of Viennese life is being a regular guest. You must take an interest in uninteresting personalities, and you have to partake of attention you do not want. The only advantage is that you are greeted by your name. You might well have forgotten it in this confusion; in any case the other regular guests will now remember it for certain.

725 One of the most awful of our barbaric eating customs is being forced to review an entree upon presentation of the bill. Here I am, already weary of life, and I have to confess to the waiter how my meat was.

726 The shortage of great men to move society forward is explained in the end by the excess of great men driving our coaches.

727 We don't need no judge to decide that Vienna is more beautiful than Berlin. But that is the sad thing.

728 Girardi in Berlin? We have made ourselves into a bazaar on the Berlin pattern, where there is no room for authenticity. That is why authenticity had to flee to Berlin. There is room for everything there, because there they have a proven system we are not ready for. We have become ethnographically interesting and have sent the essence of our folk culture off to the World Fair. The final indignity will be when the last Austrian appears in Kastan's Panoptikum.

729 The unearned beauty of this town! But those who exhort
her to the so-called seriousness of labor are as foolish as her
flatterers and Sunday magazine writers. What is lamentable
is not that her men are not working but that they are not
thinking. In fact it is meritorious to rely on the sky being
blue and the grass green. Someone who says you cannot live
on that is a Philistine. But someone who says it is sad to live
on that if you are not an artist—he speaks the truth.

730 The magic of all fantastical life and all the glimmers of fairy
tales weave themselves about a city where there are taxi
meters. A dreary barracks spirit forces us to acknowledge
once a day that the Prater is beautiful.

731 When you whiz by the monuments of a city in an automobile, they cannot get to you.

732 Hopeful seed of Berlin tastelessness! It is built for the
present and guarantees that everyone will get to renew his
dreams tomorrow. Fantasy hurries up wooden stairs and
submerges itself where it pleases. In the human melee one
comes to oneself. You are not noticed "inter alia," you disappear inter alia. Everyone is a number, so everyone has the
freedom to be a personality. Everything follows the clock, so
everyone can follow his own. Order makes life adventurous.
A comforting feeling of insecurity overcomes you. Anyone
crushed under the wheels stands up again in one piece. No
idle bystander resents you for eating oysters. Waiters talk like
statesmen and none of the guests notices them. Life goes by
in a flash, you can scarcely pursue it to the next street corner, and the moment is beautiful, because you cannot say to
it as Faust does: "Do linger, you are so beautiful." E. T. A.
Hoffmann moves out of Lutter's wine bar into the automat.
Makeup makes life authentic. These women are not alive at
all during the day, they gather together the most necessary
of their limbs to dress themselves up properly for the
evening: if half a bosom is missing, it doesn't matter.

Friedrich Street is so desolate that a fata Morgana can appear any moment . . . here in Austria the wonders of authenticity have been created once and for all and we bang our heads bloody against them.

733 It is unjust always to reproach Vienna for its faults, since its advantages also deserve blame. But B's book goes so far as to reproach Vienna for the faults that are merely missing advantages. How high the author exalts the cultural *niveau* of the Viennese, just to attack it! This false optics of blame is deplorable. It has a need to project onto a nation the advantages it wants to begrudge. The author has discovered in Austrian culture the worldview of illusion; that the Viennese lives in an unreal world he blames on a dynasty that is certainly the most faithful custodian of real property. History wanted "one test of whether the mind could rule the world alone," so it installed the Habsburgs. They created the world from their mind. To think that such panegyrics to the most sublime artistic sensibility were considered disloyal! But I will not tolerate such twisted contemplation of a national soul that exhausts itself in petty authenticities. For the world of Vienna is created not from spirit but from beef. This solidity, which measures by the kilo, ruins any imagination that could create a world. The creative spirit of unreality discovered by the author has only once had a visible hand in Austrian history: back during the laying of the Southern Railway between Vienna and Baden. It turned out there was no mountain to build the tunnel a royal highness wanted— the tunnel was built anyway.

734 In Berlin you walk on papier maché, in Vienna you bite granite.

735 In Berlin grass will not grow. In Vienna it withers.

736 Everything in Vienna clips wings! A test pilot who starts out pushing the envelope ends up sealing himself into it. From flyer to friar in one fell snip.

Eight

737   When the sun spent days scuffling with the clouds, it was like the struggle between the yellow panther and the black steer. The realities of the barometer cannot spoil the excitement of dramas like this.

738   Sunset, loneliness and three kaftans on the beach at Norderney. When the sun dips into the sea and the colors of her departure spread over the horizon, the three points mingle themselves in as though they belong to the spectrum. The immutability of things, doubly illustrated. Which is more eternal?

739   Coquetry is merely talent. But there are glances that do not say they love, only sate themselves with being loved. They have so much love because they have so much love to take in. The man out on his walk, who stops in enchantment, might believe they are for him; but they are probably for the dog, whose mistress carries him across the street in a pose unforgettable for both dog and man.

740 Two people did not marry. Since then they live in mutual widowerhood.

741 Her husband permits her to do amateur theater—la Bohème would not have allowed her to be married. So there is still more freedom in society than in la Bohème, which has its incontrovertible norms.

742 An infallible test of stupidity. I ask a servant when yesterday's visitors came. He looks at his watch and says, "I don't know, I didn't look at the clock!"

743 The dull form of humor: The passengers in an omnibus smile when someone slips while climbing off. He in turn smiles when he manages to catch himself after all.

744 If you want to try mental gymnastics, try to reconstruct as fast as possible the conversation around a dinner table, starting from the point where it dawns on you how far you have traveled from the original theme. Thumb through this conversational lexicon, and you will see a zigzag path beginning and ending with subjects whose droll miscellany might remind you of labels: From Gothicism to Central Heating and from Newton to the Pacific.

745 In doubtful cases, choose what is right.

746 The most scurrilous manifestation of human dignity: the indignant face of a waiter, when someone has banged on the table after calling out in vain.

747 An umbrella factory surrenders public taste to the sight of a billboard portraying Romulus and Remus with open umbrellas. I have often reflected on this symbolism, but always found only the same sad explanation: Due to bad weather the founding of Rome has been called off.

748 A drive to the Prater: The horse has the whole world in front of it. To the coachman the world is the size of a horse's rear end. To the cavalier the world is the size of the

coachman's back. And to the gaping populace the world has shrunk to the size of the cavalier's face.

749   What is the conscious might of a Nero, what is the annihilating will of a Genghis Khan, what is the perfected power of the Last Judgment, compared to the self-esteem of a planner at the Military Draft Board Department of the Magisterial County Hall, condemning you to a fine of two kroner for ignoring a Summons to Report for the Purpose of Assessment in Apportionment of Military Tax!

750   Better not have anything stolen. That way at least you do not have to bother with the police.

751   The violence of existence, the capriciousness of all human affairs never dawns on one so clearly as when one has the misfortune to sit in a carriage that has to stop because the music at the Burg is surging around it.

752   I saw clearly in a drunkard's walk how Sunday was one more monkey on his back.

753   I had a frightful vision: I saw a conversational lexicon approach a renaissance man and open him.

754   What a curious procession! She walks behind him like a corpse behind a mourner.

755   P.A.'s folly is the wisdom that has enough humor to question itself.

756   La Bohème has strange saints. A hermit that lives on spices!

757   Emerson: German philosophy that crossed the great water and took some on underway.

758   The new snob: The Picture of Dorry Gray.

759   The philosopher L. St. from Hungary: not a leader among thinkers, but top boy in his class. People call him to the table and he fiddles them transcendental tunes.

760 Anthologists are the busybodies of science. Premeddlers.

761 A worldview is a good horse. But still there is a difference between a rider and a horse trader.

762 An editor who always finds an opinion for the fitting words.

763 There can scarcely be another author who has so quickly become not famous as this *X*.

764 Not everyone who imagines himself a Brutus is therefore a Spiegelberg.

765 He borrowed spurs and gave free rein to someone else's megalomania.

766 He was new wine that acted absurd but wasn't.

767 Keep on plowing with the other man's calf and you end up plowing with the golden calf.

768 The bigger the rake, the bigger the pile. The bigger the booby trap, the bigger the boom. The bigger the crock, the bigger the skim. The bigger the canard, the bigger the bill. The bigger the swine, the bigger the pork. The bigger the boot, the bigger the heel.

769 He spilled my guts, vented my spleen and shot off my mouth on the most sensitive topics.

770 It was the style of the great comic Knaack: an inflammatory word spoken in jest.

771 At mealtime he doesn't let his appetite spoil his anger.

772 A superb pianist; but his playing has to drown out the after-dinner belching of respectable society.

773 Willya look at that. The Chairman of the Board of the Cretinous Corporation and the Managing Director of the Amalgamated Banality Works!

774 Landscape dramatically influences the development of the body. There are parts of the Alps where the natives have goiters and the visitors flat feet.

775 Presumably the spleen functions like a notary public; necessary but superfluous.

776 Dignity is the conditional form of the human verb.

777 His convictions meant more to him than anything, more than life itself. But he had the courage to sacrifice, and when it came down to it, he laid down his convictions for his life.

778 After getting himself thrown out of the anarchist party, there was nothing left for him to do but become a useful member of bourgeois society and join the social democrats.

779 Someone said I had tried to push his back to the wall. That is untrue. I merely succeeded.

780 A computer invested in a writer but did not cover its costs.

781 With what the heart lacketh the mouth overfloweth.

782 I dreamed that in Germany there was a mental warrior who crossed all *s*'s out from between the parts of compound words. These *s*'s are such beloved children in the German tongue that leaving them out was like removing the spaces from English phrases. He used words like *libelaction, habitualoffender, trialdate, attemptedpimping*. But the rejected "*s*" sounds decided to avenge themselves on him, and one day as he told an old man about the sexual indiscretions of his misspent youth, they all joined in a hissing chorus the likes of which had never been heard in Germany. And there was no reasontohushthemup.—As I awoke I noticed that this was all castlesintheair.

783 I knew a hero with thick skin like Siegfried and thin heels like Achilles.

784 There are people who are tolerated in pubs only because they do not pay. They are called editors.

785 Wise guys: an itchy scalp is not a brain event.

786 He envies the other fellow's humor as a young scab envies chronic eczema.

787 Contact with him is like touching mucus. Since realizing this I never touch mucus.

788 An unscrupulous painter. On the pretext of wanting to have her he lures her into his atelier and paints her.

789 She entered marriage under false pretenses. She was a virgin and did not tell him!

790 The day I would not survive: when I get sick from the thought of voting while my girlfriend spryly strides to the ballot.

791 Where she trod, no grass grew, only the dust she made her men bite.

792 Can you take a pinch of snuff from Pandora's box? To your health, Friend W!

793 He was jealous and gathered moss. He wanted his wife to live in cryptogamy.

794 The social order inclines less to heterosexuality than control-sexuality.

795 We live in a society that translates "monogamy" as "single coupon bond."

796 There are no misunderstood women. They are merely the effect of a verbal mixup that happened to a feminist. She wanted to be not understood but grasped. So there are in fact misunderstood women after all.

797 The Philistine gets drunk on the pure rotgut he pours for the girl on the subject of his assets.

798 Medicine: Your money and your life!

799 He died, bitten by the serpent of Aesculapius.

800 Modern symbol: Death with a mohawk.

801 A newspaper is canned time.

802 Since I merely skim the daily press, I happened to garble two neighboring headlines: "Iswolski's Visit to Austria" and "Attempted Robbery in Junk Shop."

803 A quotial climber emitted the necrologism: *De mortuis nil admirari.*

804 Sire, at least permit trains of thought to accept passengers until further notice!

805 Secularization. The Church has a strong stomach. Even so one should pump it out from time to time.

806 Wilhelm at Bismarck's burial: In Friedrichsruh an uninvited guest had the coffin lid slammed in his face.

807 The Germans. "Nation of bards and sages"? Cremation and bars and cages!

808 Liberalism serves dishwater as an elixir vitae.

809 Before you let life befall you, get yourself anesthetized.

Nine

810　Aphorisms are never congruent with the truth: they are either half-truths or one-and-a-half.

811　There are two types of prejudice. One is beyond all judgment. It anticipates the inner truth before judgment has approached the outer. The other is beneath all judgment: it does not approach even the outer truth. The first type is above doubting its rightness; it is too proud not to be justified, it cannot be overcome, and it leads to isolation. The second listens to reason; it makes its bearer well-liked. A judicious maneuver for prejudicial treatment.

812　Prejudice is an indispensable houseboy who turns away tedious impressions at your doorstep. You just have to make sure your houseboy doesn't throw you out as well.

813　The world has exactly the boundaries imagination gives it. Coming to terms with this shows a healthy mixture of wild fantasy and pedantry. An adjustable horizon cannot be narrow.

814 There are people who take off their winter coats in spring-time and people who view taking off their winter coats as an infallible means of inducing spring. The first group is more likely to catch cold.

815 It is not the ability to examine things analytically but the fantastical application of knowledge that undergirds all riot-ous enjoyment in kitchens and taverns, all connoisseurship in love and life. You know not whence you grow fat.

816 My senses activate my mind, the female mind activates my senses. And my body? That I think and feel away. *Experimenta in corpore vili.*

817 What are all the orgies of Bacchus compared to the intoxica-tion of the man who abandons himself to unbridled conti-nence!

818 Perfection is so limited, the forest so bald, poetry so sober! They are lessons in contemplation, for the limited, the bald, the sober.

819 Imagine how much variety there must be in someone's life when he has sat every day for twenty years at the same chair in a pub!

820 A barrel organ plays a melody for every pain.

821 Wanted: Desert suitable for fata Morgana.

822 You would not believe how hard it often is to translate a deed into a thought!

823 A self-confident artist would have called out to Fiesco: I have painted what you merely did!

824 My image of him is accurate. If he differs from it, that proves nothing about my image: the inaccuracy is in him.

825 Nothing speaks more against a theory than its practicability.

826 Hypocrites are hateful not because they practice what they preach against but because they preach what they do not practice. Whoever condemns moral hypocrisy must take the greatest pains to avoid being considered a friend of the moral code hypocrites betray. What is criminal is not betrayal of morality but morality itself. It is intrinsically hypocritical. What should be exposed is not that they drink wine but that they preach water. Documenting contradictions between theory and practice is always tricky business. What if one person's thoughts mean more than everyone else's deeds? The moralist could be serious about the struggle against an immorality he has himself fallen prey to. And when someone preaches wine, one can forgive him even for drinking water. He is living a contradiction, but he does see to it that there is more wine drunk in the world.

827 To me the least extenuating circumstance was always that the defendant couldn't help it.

828 Father, forgive them, for they know what they do!

829 I have sinned for the sake of many a good apology. So I will be forgiven.

830 Thank God I have shot so much more often above the target than beside it.

831 Earlier in life my indignation was often amoral; but decency gains ground on every front, and you give up.

832 A paradox arises when a premature insight collides with the nonsense of the times.

833 An antithesis looks like a mere mechanical inversion. But you have to build up so much capacity for experience, suffering, insight before you can invert a word!

834 Soon it will be ten years that I have not been myself. The last time I was myself I founded a polemical journal.

835 Certainly I too am a scribbler. But because of a truly irresistible compulsion. Not that any computer has yet had to sue me for overburdening it. But it is true that my fingers cannot always fulfill the orders of my head. How I envy those authors whose heads cannot fulfill the needs of their fingers! They can at least get some rest.

836 My readers believe that I write for the moment, because I write from the moment. So I have to wait until my works are outdated. Perhaps then they will be up-to-date.

837 The dominant apes of all parties have united in accusing me of preaching unchastity. Admittedly it is true that I recommended beauty as the sole remedy for stupidity, and that I traced all the evils of this world back to the cruel, centuries-long clogging up and malicious defilement of the source of all life. But does this mean I was enthusiastic about the sexuality of apes?

838 My public and I understand each other very well: it does not hear what I say, and I do not say what it wants to hear.

839 My wish that my things be read twice has aroused great bitterness. Unjustly so; the wish is modest. It is not as if I asked that they be read once.

840 People don't understand English, and I can't express myself in journalese.

841 The one concession one could still perhaps condescend to would be to follow the wishes of the public to the extent of doing their opposite. But I do not do this, because I make no concessions and write something even when the public expects it.

842 This lack of recognition is about to turn me into a megalomaniac!

843 If I am going to be hushed up, I want to make the silence audible! Not talking about it would be a lazy retort.

844 I am free enough to give myself all the happiness I could get from a coterie.

845 I can proudly say that I have spent my days and nights reading nothing, and that bit by bit, by using every free moment, my iron will is building up an encyclopedic lack of education.

846 I would have so much raw material if only there were no events!

847 The only time I can judge the aesthetic and cultural value of a parade or a certain sort of theater piece is when I was not there. Otherwise my nerves go a little haywire and I sound like a blind man talking about colors. Music bribes the critical faculties; how easily the sound of bells can lead one to tolerate a nullity! So to maintain objectivity I must remain conscientious about staying far away from the spectacle.

848 When I call a literary man a bungler, people reproach me for nourishing personal antipathies. They underestimate my complacency. I would certainly not overtax my hatred just to trash a literary nobody!

849 I carve my opponent to suit my arrow.

850 Plague and earthquake are grand themes. How petty my enemies find it to interpret rheumatism as a symptom of plague, to obsess about impurities in spring water being portents of earthquake! How petty to feel disgusted by life when some schmock passes by!

851 There are people who avoid me as if I were a wild beast. They should not do that: we distance ourselves all too far from one another as it is. For it is they whom I avoid, with much faster stride, as if they were tame house pets.

852 Why do so many people blame me? Because they praise me and I blame them anyway.

853 Someone who does not want to deal with life should post a notice that he plans to reduce his supply of acquaintances and is letting his experiences go for less than market value.

854 Over the years I have developed into a reverse social climber. I lie in wait, feel my way, hunt around, to see how I can repel an acquaintance or lose an influential connection. Perhaps I will achieve a decent position after all!

855 When someone cannot breathe the air of my character and ends up having to betray me, public opinion says: Aha! For my unreliability has been famous since the day I fled unclean air.

856 Real fidelity surrenders a friend sooner than an enemy.

857 I was seldom beguiled, always reviled.

858 Be on your guard with women! You can catch a worldview that will rot your bones.

859 Bridle your passions, but take good care not to give your reason free rein either.

860 Experiences are savings that a miser sets aside. Wisdom is an inheritance even a spendthrift cannot squander.

861 A forced lie is always forgivable. But someone who tells the truth when he is not forced to do so deserves no mercy.

862 Truth is a clumsy manservant who smashes the dishes he washes.

863 Vanity is the indispensable guardian of divine gifts. It is foolish to demand that a woman unconditionally surrender her beauty, or a man his wit, just to avoid vexing the ungifted. It is foolish to insist that something worthy not draw attention to itself, simply to avoid revealing the worthlessness of an-

other. Those who reproach me with vanity make themselves vulnerable to suspicions of envy, a far less attractive quality than vanity. But those who deny my vanity deny my gifts as well.

864 Neither female sensuality nor male artistry really needs outside fuel. The more negligible the occasion, the greater the results. The mind cannot be fettered by class prejudice, and lust possesses perspective.

865 Fantasy has a right to carouse in the shade of the trees it makes into a forest.

866 Mirroring the self is permissible when the self is beautiful. It grows into a duty when the mirror is good.

867 Every insight should cause a shock as intense as a farmer feels when he learns one day that imperial advisers and royally appointed merchants have no advice to offer the emperor and no goods to deliver to the palace. He becomes mistrustful.

868 There is a low credulity of trust and a higher credulity of skepticism. The first is merely deceived, the second is man enough to deceive itself. One is a fopling, the other is in the know but does not allow knowledge to spoil his fun when he looks back over his shoulder. (I wanted her signature on a postcard. I asked a friend to forge it. If he proceeded to write that it was real I would surely believe it). Earlier, when I still believed, I could never have imagined the scale of my own credulity. Now I am often astonished at the surprises I spring on myself, and astonished at my surprise. Since my mistrust has grown I know how deeply I believe.

869 Long after we have abandoned an error, superficial people reproach us with the error and thorough people with inconsistency.

870 A personality has a right to be wrong. The Philistine can be right wrongly.

871 The wiser man yields, but only if it was suffering that wised him up.

872 An inauthentic person does not believe in any sort of authenticity. And even if he did, he would not grasp how one could be authentic in an age when really no one needs to be.

873 At a costume ball everyone hopes to be the most outstanding, but the only person who stands out is the one with no costume. Is there not a comparison to be drawn here?

874 You have not yet found the right kind of solitude if you remain preoccupied with yourself.

875 You can despise the people who have no time. You can deplore those who have no work. But the men who have no time to work—envy them!

876 Nothing about an ideal should be attainable except martyrdom.

877 The man who smashes down open doors need not fear his windows being broken into.

878 What torments you is the lost possibilities. When you become certain of an impossibility you have made a profit.

879 No matter how I twist and turn, life shows me losses everywhere. It has either sacrificed art to practicality or practicality to art.

880 The individual life of the big apparatchiks cometh of evil. I can imagine that they have political convictions, but it disturbs me that they breathe.

881 It is unfortunate that the world contains more stupidity than wickedness requires and more wickedness than stupidity causes.

882 Thoughts are duty-free. But then there are worries.

883 True cruelty cannot be limited by any particular instrument of power.

884 Nationalism is the love that connects me to the idiots of my country, the people who libel my morals and defile my native tongue.

885 The biggest local event, the one taking place in all cities simultaneously and incessantly, gets the least attention: the invasion of spiritual life by the military.

886 It is not a proper Inner Light unless it becomes a will-o'-the-wisp for the understanding.

887 Common sense says it will "go along with" the artist up to a certain point. The artist should decline the company even that far.

888 In a poet one can observe symptoms that would mark a minister of trade as ripe for involuntary commitment.

889 The "dead letter of the law"? Life itself has frozen into a letter. What difference does the rigor mortis of legality make!

890 The serious matters of life are the toys grown-ups play with. The problem is that they cannot compare with the sensible things that fill the nursery.

891 The philosopher thinks from eternity into the moment, the poet from the moment into eternity.

892 Fencing and club swinging are treacherous therapies for flab. They create hunger and thirst. What most people lack, what would infallibly help them, is the opportunity for mental exercise.

893 Every orderly mental household should have the threshold of its consciousness thoroughly cleaned several times a year.

894 If you want a clear judgment about your friends, ask your dreams.

895 Now and again dreams bestow a bit of clarity and one is grateful to them. I dreamed of a bloated caterpillar that I wanted to kill. I stabbed at it, but it stayed alive, and turning its head to me, it smiled and said: I'll be back.

896 I know exactly which uninvited thoughts not to allow across the threshold of my consciousness.

897 I do not envy the security of the man who feels safe from all surprises in his room at night. Even if you know that pictures do not leave their frames, you can still believe it could happen. We should hold on to such a belief. It is not the belief of our forefathers, but because it is derided as the belief of children one should take it seriously. It is the heresy of superstition. There is no need to accede to the dogma that you should not do thirteen bad deeds on a Friday. But the door latch I grabbed with my left hand will stand up and bear witness against me!

898 If you have settled into a personal relationship with the things in your room, you are not eager to move them from their places. I would sooner buy a new book than lend one from my library. I do not like lending books even to myself. An unread book right at hand is worth more to me than a read one somewhere else.

899 I much prefer to believe that the magician's art can be explained only in metaphysical fashion. Otherwise it would be even more inexplicable. For all I know a skillful trickster could manage to fit a bunny rabbit, three doves and a ribbon one hundred meters long into my hat. But what I cannot explain in terms of natural causes is how he got them all into his pocket.

900 When I am going to sleep, I clearly feel the moment when the shutter of consciousness closes. This opens it up again for a moment. But it is just the reassurance that consciousness is ebbing. A kind of imprimatur of sleep.

901 Someone who wants to sleep and cannot is more powerless than someone who must sleep but does not want to. The second fellow has the excuse of a natural law, though admittedly he can thwart it with black coffee. The insomniac has to resort to a good conscience or, if that does not work, a German novel or ultimately morphine. These are not worthy medicines. Human nature is outranked by sleep; since it cannot outrank sleep, it must learn to outwit it. You draw your favorite figures in the air, you insist on taking the most absurd toys to bed: a calf with eight feet, a face with the tongue hanging out of its forehead, or the elf-king with his crown and his train. You arrange for the disorder the god of sleep requires before he will even consider getting involved with the likes of us. With a little skill you can pull an inconceivable number of ribbons, rabbits and other irrelevant things out of the magic hat of the unconscious. Nothing impresses Sleep more. In the end he believes in them, and the magician has disappeared beneath all the knickknacks. I have often conducted the experiment wide awake, and it was so successful that I was not around to confirm its success.

902 One way you can tell you are highly strung: the first moment you lie down in bed, you feel the previous night's dream, but no more distinctly than a lunar landscape feels a veil of fog.

903 Immediately after a lecture on the occurrences of Encolopius I dreamed, one after another, all the astronomical portents that Petronius describes as premonitions of civil war: I saw comets; bloody rain fell; "streams stood dying in their courses." But Aetna, which spews billows of fire from its guts, was the sundial. I was already hopeful—but the Vi-

ennese public, in the Hotel Panhans, thought nothing of it. They sat on the terrace and applauded each heavenly omen. I was outraged by the shameless disturbance of the wonderful spectacle and thought to myself: that is really Roman. Clearly Petronius's portrayal of the Romans' impudent haughtiness set the tone for this polemical part of the dream: "Rome had already conquered the globe. . . ." Tigers were let loose on humans, "to drink their fill of blood, while the Romans happily chatted away about it."

904 What could be more charming than the suspense of wondering how the place I have imagined so often will really look? The suspense of wondering how I will restore my image of it after I have actually seen it.

905 For many years now I have missed spring. But in exchange I have it at all seasons, as soon as I can call forth from within myself the mood of a childhood day, with its abrupt transition from the multiplication table to a garden scent of larkspurs and caterpillars. Since I suspect that there are no more of these, I assiduously avoid further personal experience in this matter.

906 Reviving the imaginative life of a childhood day ought to be an enticing prospect. The peach tree in the courtyard, which was then quite big, has now become very small. The Laudon hill was a Chimborazo. The trick is to scale these things back up to the dimensions of childhood. Sometimes fantasy manages it momentarily before you fall asleep. Suddenly everything is there again. The head on your fox fur duvet becomes quite scary; the dog barks in the next villa; and a wave of schoolroom memories carries along a scent of graphite, with the echo of the song "Young Siegfried Wa-a-as a Brave Hero": the teacher bowing the fiddle as if he were Volker in the flesh; the old beating of the heart because you might "get it" if you were bad; larkspur blossoming in the garden; milk warm from the cow; the first equation in one

unknown, the first meeting with a girl unknown; the swimming master calling out the rhythm; cholera in Egypt, the skittishness about seeing in the newspaper the names of the towns Damiette and Rosette (each with two hundred dead per day)—they could bring contagion; the smell of a stuffed squirrel; in the distance a barrel organ playing new releases like "Only For Nature" or "He Should Be Your Lord." All this in half a minute. Anyone unable to summon all this at will is entitled to a refund on his school fees. A good brain must be capable of imagining every bout of childhood fever in such detail that it gets a temperature.

907 A world of sweet sound has sunk into time, and all that remains on the program is a crowing rooster.

908 Shortly before falling asleep you can draw all sorts of grimaces in the air. These are hypnagogic faces. If you see an entire human body, you are close to leaving this world.

909 Day of horror, lying there trampled by the horses' hooves of stupidity, with no help anywhere in sight!

910 Resorting to reflection, out of sheer world-weariness: a suicide one uses to give oneself life.

911 "Having no more illusions": that is when they really begin.

912 As long as you have inner covering, losses in the external world have nothing on you.

913 One should allow oneself time for all things, except the eternal things.

914 Immortality is the only thing that cannot tolerate postponement.

915 You often have to figure out what you are happy about; but you always know what you are sad about.

916 I have observed that the butterflies are dying out. Or are they only seen by children? When I was ten years old, I

mingled only with admirals on the meadows of Weidlingau. I can say that it was the proudest phase of my social career. Mourning-cloaks, peacock and brimstone butterflies too brought color to a young life. *Vanessa io, Vanessa cardui— vanitas vanitatum!* When I returned after many years, they had all disappeared. The midday sun blazed as before, but there were no shimmering colors to be seen; instead there were shreds of newspaper on the meadow. Later I learned they had used the wood from the forests to make printing paper. With such an abundance of information the butterflies had to remain expendable. A friend of our journal sends us "the last butterfly," and one of our colleagues had the opportunity to spear one on his pen and ask him why he had become so isolated. The world flees before the colors of personality, protecting itself by organizing. Only the butterflies have failed to organize. Thus it came to be editors and brilliant Sunday magazine writers who now taste the calyxes. Even the monotone cabbage white butterfly, which had a certain affinity with the journalists and could thus most easily have come to terms with them, had to give way. The war to annihilate the flying creatures marks the triumph of newspaper culture. Butterflies and women, beauty and wit, nature and art are made painfully aware that a Sunday paper has 150 pages. Humanity whacks at the butterflies with flyswatters. Washes the colored dust from its fingers, for they must be clean to touch printer's black.

917 If only Nature would finally grow dark! This miserable twilight will ruin our eyes yet.

918 You don't even live once.

The Twist: *Dicta and Contradicta* in Context

JONATHAN MCVITY

Karl Kraus descended to Hell, to judge the living and the dead.
—OSKAR KOKOSCHKA

Imagine you learn one day that without warning professors of the Sorbonne have nominated you for the Nobel Prize in literature. You might think this would make interesting news copy in your own country, somewhere. But there is never a word on the news or in the papers. The entire media establishment is so livid with envy that it can scarcely bear to admit you even exist. This actually happened to the monumental twentieth-century Viennese media critic and satirist Karl Kraus.

Kraus embodied Goethe's dictum that the highest example of each type transcends its type: from the decaying Austro-Hungarian Empire to the Third Reich he pressed ephemeral satire and commentary across the border into the aphoristic outskirts of philosophy and got to spend immortality with the likes of Sébastien Roch Nicolas Chamfort (1741–94). Despite his independent wealth and extravagant personality he created an arsenal of lasting mental weapons and poetic barriers against manipulative mediocrity and complacent brutality.

He became Viennese at the age of three after his family moved from Jecin in Bohemia, where he was born April 28, 1874, the ninth of ten children. His father was a humorous and sarcastic manufacturer, inventor of the paper bag, who made his first fortune using Bohemian prison labor and then moved to conventional manufacturing. The elder Kraus sailed unharmed through repeated stock market crashes, while his son vainly warned his readers before both world wars.

For thirty-seven years, beginning on April Fools' Day 1899, Karl Kraus wrote much or all of the voluminous journal he edited and published. He chose to call it *Die Fackel* (The torch) after toying with *The Lantern,* which Victor Henri Rochefort had used several decades earlier for his iconoclastic journal. After abortive attempts as an actor, Kraus had begun his career writing for a variety of newspapers and magazines and saw them all as instruments of corruption. He was also more than disillusioned with the self-conscious fin-de-siècle decadence of the Impressionist "Young Vienna" literary clique at the Griensteidl, the "Cafe Megalomania."

Linguistic corruption was to remain his lifelong nemesis. He believed social corruption depended on dishonest language: venal literature and meretricious mass media, subtly usurping human critical faculties by palming off judgments as facts. Through the *Fackel* he would drag dishonesty into the light of day while setting a positive counterexample of a German language pure enough to resist warping by warmongers, profiteers, and poseurs: a medium worthy of the highest art, faithful to the greatness of Goethe. No more glib opinion mongering and neologism as with Heinrich Heine, who he insisted had given German the "French disease."[1] As a tiny boy with curvature of the spine, Kraus had complained to his teacher about being weak in German. Now his polemical war cry was "It's not what we state, it's what we devastate," and that teacher was to dub him "Satiricus Satiricorum."[2]

His best-known weapon was wordplay. He was a genius at concealing very general social criticism in humorous, often scandalous double meanings. These were so subtle and numerous that even readers of his time and place did not always grasp them, and they often strenuously resist translation: an extreme species of *Dichtung,* the German word that equates literary art with the "densifying," the "packing" or concentration of experience and thought. Kraus saw his wordplay in the tradition of the German Romantics Ludwig Tieck and Jean Paul (Johann Paul Friedrich Richter's pseudonym), as well as Johann Nestroy.

From the start the *Fackel* was sold out at thirty thousand copies and was carried about by intellectuals and rebels all over Austria, Germany, Hungary, and beyond. Conceived in Kraus's inside-out combination of daytime sleep with nighttime commentary on the daytime excesses of industrious idiocy, it created a personality cult amplified by the 701 readings Kraus gave to generally sold-out houses, combining his own material with that of Shakespeare, Goethe, Nestroy, Wedekind, Hauptmann, Schiller, Baudelaire, Strindberg, Aristophanes, and more. Though he could not sing, he was known to chant the operettas of Jacques Offenbach, whom he called "the greatest satirical creator of all times and cultures."[3] Audience veneration was often one-sided; Kraus bluntly refused to humor his fans, and in the end the *Fackel* ignored not just legal and critical attacks but all correspondence.

He donated the proceeds of readings and copyright-infringement settlements to homeless shelters and low-cost housing, desperate friends, Quakers caring for starving tubercular children, and the like. He forced a psychoanalytical group to donate the proceeds of their illicit Kraus aphorism edition to the poet Else Lasker-Schueler, who "although she does far more for mankind, earns from her own dreams not nearly as much as a psychoanalyst does with those of others."[4] It was Kraus who inspired Ludwig Wittgenstein to fund a trust for struggling artists. When bankruptcy overtook a friend's theater troupe, he helped cover the outstanding debt. He took no income from the *Fackel* and accepted little advertising, setting its price to cover only production and the stipends of the many distinguished collaborators, from Hugo von Hofmannsthal and Heinrich Mann to Oscar Wilde,

August Strindberg, and the departed Otto Weininger. The artist had an intrinsic ethical responsibility, unlike the mere aesthete who had the same relation to beauty as "the pornographer to love or the politician to life."[5]

Yet contradiction was a way of life with Kraus, challenging the translator to construct a correspondingly brilliant English persona entitled to constant assault on the foundations of social life. He demanded every inch of the high moral ground while reserving the right to play Viennese Wycherley or Rochester: at one extreme a self-tormenting linguistic philosopher enamored with chastity, taking toys to bed, tiring of life because he found a typo, calling the divine word the father to the thought, reviling the hacks who pimp it; at another extreme a libertine crediting the pimp with the virtue of matrons and the whore with the brilliance of the Greeks. A successful publisher—a media critic, no less—accusing his daily newspapers of stripping the biosphere. A Christian convert touting betrayal as most of the fun in adultery, mocking Christian sexual ethics as the Judas kiss, as a poison cocktail, or as Don Quixote trailed by the Sancho Panza of syphilis. An incurable lover of a city whose culture was rich enough even to pave the streets but whose beauty was unearned, whose virtues deserved blame as much as its faults, whose petty authenticities rested on beef rather than spirituality, where it was rude to think, where life slowed to a crawl and even the machines refused to work on Sundays, where cabbies and waiters all thought themselves heroes and military bureaucrats fancied themselves vaster than Genghis Khan.

Most conspicuous in the feminized century, Kraus was a professed admirer of women who stated in so many words that male virtues were illnesses in women, who laughed at the imposture that chromosomes and hormones could be legislated out of existence, who vacillated between denying females even sexual charm and openly frequenting prostitutes, who trampled maternity and childhood just as readily as he did honor, and morality, and the humdrum "Drahn" of bourgeois normality, and patriotism, fraternity, equality, gratitude, coeducation, classical liberalism, public affairs, humanitarianism, and human rights.

To someone looking back from the era of automated nonconformity, the organic variety might seem a gratuitous overdose. But behind the relentlessness of the satire were literary analogues of the "falsificationism" and "epistemological anarchism" poles in later Viennese expatriate philosophy of science.

On the one hand, all useful ideas are mortal, and the best you can do is condense and test them as hard as possible to reduce error in the next version. Frontal attack on the principle of press freedom is blatantly paradoxical coming from the independent publisher of the *Fackel,* and no subscriber to the U.S. Bill of Rights could ultimately endorse it even from a less contradictory source; yet without the invigoration of such radical attack the principle atrophies to a sacred cow, a front for media concentration and Mosca's "permanent campaign." Kraus might have been irritated by the label, but this is critical rationalism; he called it routine cleaning at the threshold of consciousness. Similarly with his contempt for parliamentarianism, capable of degenerating into a fig leaf for plutocracy or the "national security state."

On the other hand, left to its own devices, the orthodoxy of reason stupefies humanity more than any religion does; the specter of Swift's Houyhnhnms requires periodic exorcism, digressions into apparent childishness, delta states, superstition. Reason had outfitted industrial society for the mass production of stupidity, fraud, and mediocrity on a scale it might never be able to flush from its blood. The power of the weapons was wildly out of proportion to the deserts of the characters pulling the triggers. The louche pleasures of "information" threatened not merely environmental devastation but ubiquitous militaristic spiritual infection far worse than syphilis. Humankind would one day sacrifice itself to machines that could harness weasel talk to mass-produce diabolically faulty clones of every noble idea. The endless battle was to kill, falsify the intellectual mutants masquerading as genuine humanitarianism, feminism, justice.

The *Fackel* named names; Kraus believed that the battle against corruption was a personal battle. Criticizing the sin while sparing the sinner he thought was the cowardly task of the establishment press, sparing potential advertisers. For his uncompromising honesty, he was physically attacked more than once, even challenged to a duel by an angry brother. The first *Fackel* parody appeared within two months, and his enemies did everything they could to degrade and discredit him, stifling him with silence, confiscating several editions, blasting him for muckraking in the wrong waters and "demonstrating the nothingness of nullities,"[6] trying to trivialize him into a punster or mechanical inverter of proverbs, ridiculing him on the stage and in print with such names as Benjamin Abhorchent, Dalai Lama, Shallowmay, Lumpenintellectual, fartcatcher. They got legal revenge when in the course of defending a young author, Rudolf Holzer, Kraus accused the freemason journalist and reviewer Hermann Bahr of being in cahoots with a producer and accepting free land from him. At the resulting slander trial, Holzer went to pieces and fainted, and the plaintiffs managed to convince the court that negotiations had been ongoing. Kraus was crushed, "trampled by the horses' hooves of stupidity."[7]

Amidst the hypocrisies of mercenary marriage and prostitution flourishing in Vienna at the turn of the century, Kraus had become a notorious advocate of female sexual freedom, despite his notorious skepticism about bluestockings. The most perfect Vienna was the linguistic palace of Heinrich Laube's Burgtheater; the most perfect woman was the great actress; and the love of Kraus's life was the ravishing actress Annie Kalmar, whose pictures on his desk and walls were more conspicuous even than Oskar Kokoschka's Kraus portraits. She died of tuberculosis and cancer just as Kraus was racing from the Bahr trial by train to surprise her at what was to be her triumphant Hamburg debut. On her sickbed she had received a copy of a Viennese column slandering her as a spendthrift debauchee.

Heartbreak made Kraus suspend publication of the *Fackel* and spend three anonymous months in Norway. He was to love again, but he visited Kalmar's grave religiously until the day he died and provided for its further care in his will. When a friend belittled their relationship decades later, Kraus immediately cut him and blackened his name to the end. He never got over his extreme outrage at the exploitation of Kalmar's death and developed a hatred for state and media organs sucking money from interference in the extreme delicacy of sexual life: "So that's settled: sexual intercourse shall be abolished in Austria."[8] He publicly defended a woman accused of adultery against her cruel and mercenary husband, and before a huge crowd he shamed a comic from the establishment press who had revealed his relationship with the Serbian queen in her prostitute days. He castigated the English for their destruction of Wilde and demanded unconditional withdrawal of all interference with consensual pleasure of any kind. When in the novel *Ezechiel der Zugereiste* (Ezekiel the newcomer) Fritz Wittels had parodied him as "Benjamin Abhorchent,"[9] Kraus won a big judgment against the work, not on his own behalf but for libeling and violating the doctor-patient confidentiality of Irma Karczewska, a mistress he had shared with his dying friend Ludwig von Janokowski.

Kraus's eroticism does not sit well with all feminists, since it superficially resembles the travesty of sexual liberation where mass media condition women to confuse disposability with autonomy. This resemblance is dispelled by Kraus's relations with such intellectual women as Else Lasker-Schueler and Princess Lichnowsky, "more brilliant than all German writers together."[10] His revulsion at female bluestockings is a variant of his much greater revulsion at male bluestockings. This is not unrelated to the Christian sentiment that it is less diabolical to prostitute the body than the intellect and to H. L. Mencken's warning to women not to take it for granted that the climb to the top of the male professions would be worth the trouble. His handful of naughty French pictures has been taken as evidence of a sex problem, but Lasker-Schueler said Kraus understood women so well he could use them as his many-colored glass to view the world;[11] he was the true Don Juan who superficially hates women to the extent he cannot live without them.

Karl Kraus, circa 1915. Photo by Hermann Schieberth.

Courtesy of the Vienna Public Library, Manuscript Collection, Wiener Stadt- und Landesbibliothek (Handschriftensammlung).

Karl Kraus, 1920. Photo by Princess Mechtilde Lichnowsky.

From the Historical Museum of the City of Vienna, courtesy of the City of Vienna Museum Directorate. 96625/42

Karl Kraus, circa 1930.

From the Historical Museum of the City of Vienna, courtesy of the City of Vienna Museum Directorate. 133.346/1

Annie Kalmar on stage.

Courtesy of the Photographic Archive of the Austrian National Library, Vienna. FOTO: Bildarchiv, ÖNB Wien, 613.667B.

Baroness Sidonie Nádherný von Borutin.

Courtesy of the Vienna Public Library, Manuscript Collection. Wiener Stadt- und Landesbibliothek (Handschriftensammlung).

Many accused Kraus of knee-jerk harshness, negativism, mega-lomania; and even long after he announced "the Fall of the Fack-el" in 1905, planning to renounce the "delights of fuming moral wrath" in favor of more purely literary extravagance,[12] his attacks did sometimes go beyond the pale, as in his perennial vendetta against Bahr. He was in no position to throw stones at writers for their bourgeois opulence; "goût juif" is a polemical gauntlet, hardly proof that Hofmannsthal had descended from their school-boy alliance into philistinism; not all psychoanalytic explanation is reduction; dismissing the author of the *Magic Mountain* with a one-line accusation of snobbery is preposterous; French is not a disease. Also some of Kraus's positions smell of the lamp, intellec-tual five-finger exercises dressed as concert pieces: dismissing op-era altogether because operetta admits its absurdity more readily, equating scholarship with pedantry, defining the bluestocking and the courtesan as mutually exclusive, writing off the entire fallout from adultery and promiscuity. Kraus did not give alms in secret; he published his donations, though he was partly forced to when the media blackballed such deserving groups as the Quakers for associating with him. Malicious pleasure remains the most diaboli-cal of human emotions, and Kraus was not above it or above dirty tricks, such as his successful attempt to trick the newspaper editors into printing nonsensical earthquake analysis from a nonexistent mining engineer. An editor may well be a nepotist, a mercenary, a nouveau riche poseur, even a criminal warmonger, but this cannot be proven simply by stressing that he is not an engineer and may be too swamped to notice a joke.

Such objections are mainly academic in the context of the aph-orisms. Most often the victim is anonymous or forgotten, only the principle remains, and Kraus's unconscious hypocrisy or vengeful-ness only proves him guilty of original sin. His immoralism may not attain the Olympian heights of Friedrich Nietzsche's note-books, pondering whether "genetic agenda" is really less illusory than "consciousness"; but just as plainly he was no mere sniper or "ape of Zarathustra," and he avoided Nietzsche's higher-overhead contradiction of an aristocracy peopled with nonexistent selves. If he misunderstood Edvard Munch, he defended a number of equally significant new artists. He was in Berlin at the premiere rehearsals of the *Threepenny Opera* and wrote the second verse of the "Jealousy Duet" for Bertolt Brecht. Arnold Schoenberg's alliance with Kraus began long before the *Fackel* or the tone row; he sent Kraus a copy of the *Theory of Harmony* with a dedication he paraphrased as "I have perhaps learned more from you than one really ought if one wishes to remain independent. . . ."[13] Kraus printed brilliant poems by poor institutionalized lunatics, though these were later discovered to be products more of memory than of imagination. Without falling into Luddite excess, he valiantly combated the accelerating transformation of human into machine appendage, of forest into feuilleton, of sales region into battlefield. And his paradoxes were not mere exercises; his will asked his relatives not to intrude on the "private affair" of his funeral.[14]

When the world war came, he was at first quiet by design. Only lowlifes could fail to be struck dumb by horror so unnameable, by deeds so "unspeakable . . . Expect no word of mine."[15] He was also crazy with fear of losing Sidonie Nádherný von Borutin. Her Castle Janovice in Bohemia had been the setting for Kraus's first readings aloud from Shakespeare in the modest paperback editions published by Reklam. Feeling oppressed as her brother's ward and troubled by such friends as Rainer Maria Rilke who disapproved of her relationship with Kraus, she had left for Rome, planning to escape into a marriage of convenience with Count Guicciardini. The plan dissolved once the Italians joined the fray, and Kraus, unfit for normal military service, began to fight tooth and nail against the "chlorious war,"[16] the "technoromantic adventure,"[17] using every linguistic trick he knew to thwart the censors, standing in their office for hours to get just a few more commentaries and satirical collages through, reciting the enemy's Shakespeare. He was wild with outrage when war profiteers from Berlin came for pretentious state visits to the graves of his friends. The army denounced him as a defeatist, and he was not cleared until 1918. This was also the year Nádherný left him, having seen him through the creation of his major dramatic work, *Die letzten*

Tage der Menschheit (The last days of mankind), an apocalyptic montage of militaristic facticities for "Martian theater."[18] She married a doctor but divorced him and periodically reconciled with Kraus starting in 1920.

In Kraus's lifetime the Austrian press—the country's first mass media—was openly divided into camps of liberal Jews and anti-Semites, both more powerful than they would have been in a country whose political institutions were stronger relative to big media stakeholders. Vienna was the focal point of the "Jewish question," and the press was the focal point of many lives. Because Kraus opposed both camps, he was long reviled in some quarters as an anti-Semite, a quintessential "self-hating Jew." His near-mystical belief in the power of linguistic purity is faith in the Word as opposed to the graven image, yet like so many distinguished Jews he was alienated from his people. This may have begun in the twelfth grade when Kraus lost his usual position at the head of the class because his crudely Orthodox religion teacher downgraded him for questioning dogma; the culprit appears by name in the first *Fackel*. Although saying little about the theology of Judaism's "Mosaic mosaic," he came to despise what he saw as the cheap, unearned agnosticism of "literary swindlers" among his ambitious cohorts,[19] as if they had declared independence from God. They were worse than the anti-Semitic press when they applied greater intelligence to equally amoral ends. He accused Anselm von Rothschild of stealing, and it took him many years to renounce the widespread image of Theodor Herzl's Zionism as the pose of a man basically content with the status quo. He thought Jews had not really been a nation for a long time and should physically assimilate by intermarriage and nominal conversion. Repeatedly refusing nominations to Zionist congresses, he officially renounced Judaism in 1899, but he did not convert to Christianity until 1911 and very seldom discussed his conversion until he had left the church in 1923. He could not bear a church being profaned as a stage for a Hofmannsthal play. Also, the Italians had just awarded the Mother of God the Medal of Honor.

All politics and nationalism disgusted Kraus. In this he was in-

fluenced by Arthur Schopenhauer and Friedrich Nietzsche, who
abandoned national pride to those who deserved no other pride.
In a 1913 *Fackel* he endorsed nearly verbatim Schopenhauer's mo-
narchical skepticism toward the project of governing creatures,
most of whom are extremely egotistical, inconsiderate, deceitful,
even malicious, and intellectually inferior in the bargain. Because
of such aristocratic alliances, malice has sometimes overempha-
sized his parallels with various forms of reactionary nostalgia. This
is unfair to Kraus's position on technocracy, his express endorse-
ment of enlightenment over revelation and of the herd over herd-
slaughterers. Kraus was not longing for Versailles. He traveled by
plane. He owned a car and went on motor tours all over Europe,
particularly with Nádherný and her Irish governess. His 1932 reworking of Shakespeare's *Timon* was not only for the stage but also
for radio. He occasionally yielded to hope in a working class unpol-
luted by pseudoculture. After the war he endorsed the Social Democratic party as the one party that had not unconditionally sup-
ported the bloodshed, and several times professed himself honored
to lecture for free before proletarian audiences. Though it would
be crazy to lump him in with the Marxists, much less with the So-
viet Communists—their radio stations descended to dance music
too—he lent support to Marx's notorious position that real-world
Jewry cum "Judaicized Christianity" needed to transcend obses-
sion with money and status. Like the prophets, he called down the
wrath of Jehovah on Jews he accused of dragging down their
adopted culture by worshiping false gods, of being no better than
Germans in their greed and Chosen People arrogance, of striking
Bolshevik poses to cover up their past complicity in arms deals.

This ended in personal tragedy when the linguistic vices he had
spent his life reproaching individually in his fellow Jews appeared
collectively in Hitler et al. Some of his positions appeared, gene-
altered, in *Mein Kampf*; Hitler even used the term *journaille*,[20]
very likely in the belief that Kraus had coined it instead of bor-
rowing it from Alfred von Berger.[21] With the blackest irony of his
life Kraus was to concede that humanism had been cuckolded by
the German language: "Nothing occurs to me on the subject of

Hitler."[22] Most excruciatingly, some of his works were not banned by the Nazis when they came to power.

This although he had been condemning Hitler in print since 1923. The Nazis hated him as the epitome of the left-wing Jew troublemaker. They had tried to ban a performance of the epilogue from *Die letzten Tage der Menschheit* in 1924, and in 1928 the *Völkischer Beobachter* (People's observer) insisted his *Traumstück* (Dream play) be banned in Munich for mocking military glory.[23] Hitler was offended by the "tumescent pacifism and smutty cynicism," the "circumcised" perspective evident in the "typically Jewish phraseology."[24] The paper demanded the chief of police take a stand. Did he intend to do his duty, or would it be necessary to resort to other means? The question answered itself when Nazis threw stink bombs in the theater.

Kraus won the ensuing lawsuit, but the play was closed anyway, and someone reading the *Fackel*'s mail in the ensuing years might have been increasingly haunted by Kraus's description of Austria as "research lab for the Apocalypse."[25] An anonymous sample from 1930: "Kiss my ass a thousand times, Karl Kraus. . . . Hopefully the time is not far off when your carly krausy lousy skull will be crushed and totally smashed, whereupon the bits of your syphilitic brain will go flying to the four winds as a warning to your accursed and infested race, which has infected all Europe . . . it would be a pity to waste money putting a bullet through your infested body, you son of a whore, they should hang your butt on the first streetlamp in the Ringstrasse . . . done all kosher, so the Vienna pig Jews can make a long day's feast of it and all drop dead together . . . you hysterical Jewish sow, Jewish pig-dog. . . ."[26]

By the time Hitler came to power, Kraus's relations with the mainstream Left in the Social Democratic party had disintegrated. This had begun in the middle 1920s when Kraus launched a battle against the blackmailing Hungarian press baron Imre Bekessy, but the Left withheld its support for years until Bekessy accused one of its leaders of pederasty. Later the right wing of the National Guard got off lightly after murdering several members of the left-wing Guard. This led to a demonstration that turned into a battle between civilian partisans, with numerous Left deaths. Kraus called for the resignation of the police chief, but the Left reconciled with the chief; Kraus accused them of driving their fringe into the arms of the Communists. While he abhorred the growing alliance of Austrian conservatives and Nazis, the only person who seemed truly to grasp the threat from Germany was the ultraconservative Christian Socialist Engelbert Dollfuss.

In February 1933, a few months after his final German appearance, Kraus was diagnosed with the "flu," an early sign of heart disease. He told Brecht that "the rats are boarding the sinking ship."[27]

Later that year Brecht, likening himself to the customs officer who convinced Lao Tsu to write down his linguistic doctrine before leaving the country, urged Kraus to finish and publish his theories on language. But Kraus had developed an oddly persistent vein inflammation. He was stunned and disorientated by the gargantuan triumph of stupidity, yet he was unable to renounce former enmities, "for national socialism did not annihilate the press; rather: the press created national socialism."[28] Its "unchaste" cant had fatally compromised the intellectual immune system of society.[29] He cursed the Left's leadership for "losing the peace" by underestimating the blonde beast, sometimes even muddling Hitler with the dictatorship of the proletariat; and he said there was more humanity in Offenbach than in any of the social panaceas making the rounds in the totalitarian era.[30]

Deadlock in Parliament had become so intense that it suspended itself in 1933, and Dollfuss gambled on replacing the party system with a nonpartisan Fatherland Front. This was not simply for love of the corporate state; at this stage, solidarity with Mussolini was the most practical check Austria could place on Hitler's southern appetites. Kraus's game was too deep for his leftist critics in safe or Czech exile. He hoped pathetically that by pitting black against brown fascism Catholic authoritarianism could serve Austria as a kind of cowpox vaccination against the Nazi smallpox, "the triple alliance of drivel, devices and death . . . a type of human . . . which has grasped liberty only as the right to devour one another. . . ."[31] And Dollfuss did criminalize the Austrian Nazi party, now openly terrorist. To deprive Hitler of any pretext for aggression, he forced the Austrian media to report Nazi political mayhem as unsolved civil murder. All the Left really saw in all this was its old opponent, the right wing of the Guard, on the rampage. Black was brown, and besides this was all nothing more than a brief symptom of imminent capitalist implosion. Kraus was a monster to "change sides" when he needed only to raise his trusty pen to save all Europe from madness. Meanwhile the propaganda machine of Joseph Goebbels (rumored to possess a complete series of the *Fackel*) was grinding out sob stories about the common plight of innocent Nazi "tourists" and Social Democrats in Austria.

While enemies old and new smeared Kraus as a corrupt provincial featherweight, he was frantically busy immortalizing the witches' sabbath of the Third Reich in his *Die dritte Walpurgisnacht* (Third walpurgis night or Third witches' sabbath), a milestone attack on Nazi neuphemism and perfidy, playing off the classical and romantic Walpurgis Nights in Goethe's *Faust*. He intended this as a legacy, to be judged in saner times (by people with photographic memories for *Faust II* and Shakespeare). Normally Kraus wrote in tiny, illegible handwriting, which only two typesetters at Jahoda and Siegel could read; now he consented to use a Dictaphone so that the whole staff could set the type. Even as he did so, he realized that at this late stage it would just get readers arrested and would have to be suppressed. Prince Lobkowicz is rumored to have smuggled one version to London in the diplomatic bag of the Czech exile government; others went to Nádherný and to the United States via Switzerland.

Marcel Ray had translated Kraus aphorisms into French as early as 1913, and he and Kraus never gave up their correspondence. Kraus often visited France, though he had a blind spot for some of its cultural achievements and miscalculated badly in the Dreyfus affair. He lamented to Ray that disasters were piling up so fast there was no point writing. If you addressed politics, then by the time you were finished analyzing one evil another had already taken its place; you might as well have issued a polemic against a corpse. If you retreated to timeless subjects, people would not listen because their brains were too drenched with current events.

Brecht understood Kraus's silence and worried about him, issuing invitations to join him in safe Denmark and sending envoys to inquire after him. In May 1933 Kraus had extended his passport to include the United States, but in the end he could not abandon his adopted city, his German-speaking world, where in 1934 his friends threw a sixtieth birthday celebration, including the premiere of his film, *Karl Kraus: Ans Eigenen Schriften* (Karl Kraus reads from his works).

That July he was sick in bed when a friend arrived to announce the Nazis' assassination of Dollfuss. Kraus refused to believe this without corroboration, but since he did not have a radio of his own, he had to hear the grim broadcast by telephone from the Fackel Press.

Nazi infiltration swiftly eliminated all barriers to the barbarism Kraus had seen coming ten years earlier, worse "than Nietzsche's Antichrist."[32] Nádherný came to fetch him at the train one night and found him speechless, in tears. He considered not returning to Vienna.

The Fackel Press had been financially hemorrhaging since 1931. The rupture with the Left had hurt circulation so much that his reworking of Shakespeare's sonnets was advertised by postcard "in place of an advertisement in the Fackel, whose appearance is delayed." Investors had rejected a plan to expand Kraus's "Theater of Poetry" into an ensemble, and readings now had to be packed with free tickets.

In the summer of 1935 Kraus realized he had lost 50 percent of his swimming stamina in just one year, and on Goethe's birthday he drafted his will, containing errors that show a curious inability to face mortality. At his final public reading that November 11, he likened European power to a worm creeping away from the foot about to stomp it. From then on he read by invitation only, though his readings manager, Richard Lanyi, displayed the lists in his bookstore. Reviewers and Social Democrats were non grata.

That Christmas Berthold Viertel made a special trip from Hyde

Park to plumb Kraus's political state of mind. They argued all night, to no avail. Viertel was shocked at Kraus's hopelessness, as if his friend had already imagined the violent extent of things to come. He marveled at the seeming contradiction between Kraus's personal courage in refusing Kansas asylum and the political "pusillanimity of the isolated man,"[33] the anti-Austrian turned mere-Austrian, concerned only with preserving his last little corner of true German culture. Kraus for his part had taken mortal offense at the English insistence on punishing Mussolini's Abyssinian adventurism. By spiting the dictator over this minor prize England had driven him into bed with Hitler.

In the final *Fackel* of February 1936, after 922 issues and 30,000 pages, Kraus wondered whether it might prove more courageous to have attacked freedom in the past than to attack Nazism in the present. The courage required to save your own skin from the Nazi running after you is not strictly intellectual; sounding the alarm about the correlativity of liberal technocapitalism and Nazism had sent him to virtual Siberia.

That month Kraus was run over by a careless bicyclist. This greatly increased the frequency of the severe headaches that had plagued him all his life. Friends were frightened by the unprecedented memory lapses. In May 1936, a month after his final reading, he fell ill in Prague. His last written words to Nádherný on June 8 were, "The worldlies' unwisdom makes all work other than Shakespeare impossible."[34] Two days later he suffered a heart attack in the Cafe Imperial. The next day a telegram about his "hopeless" condition went out to Nádherný in Bohemia, which he had never stopped regarding as his native land. She left immediately by car, arriving eight hours before the final massive heart attack with cerebral apoplexy, at 4 A.M. on June 12.

At his deathbed was Helene Kann, whom he had met in 1904 with her sister, Elisabeth Reitler. In 1917 Reitler had killed herself in horror over the war, and from then on Kann had been Kraus's close ally, though his will forbade her to see the Kraus-Nádherný letters before publication. Among Kraus's bequests to Kann was a pillow from Annie Kalmar.

When the dying Kraus complained deliriously about the doctor, Kann, thinking he was past really understanding, said, "Oh, Karl, you're doing him an injustice too." To her shock, Kraus suddenly sat bolt upright and glared at her with his old intensity, saying, "Whom did I ever do an injustice?"[35]

Shortly before losing consciousness for the last time, he pressed the doctor for confirmation that he would be able to visit Nádherný in two days. The doctor replied yes, "I promise you, on Tristan's honor." To which Kraus responded, "To hell with that."[36]

Since Nádherný's relations with Kraus had been ambiguous in later years, not everyone had expected her at the funeral on June 15, but she appeared. Just before they started filling the grave, she tossed in a ring. She withdrew from society, never leaving Janovice until the SS chased her out to convert it into a tank factory. After the Communist takeover of Czechoslovakia, she left to die in England in 1950.

The obituaries for Kraus filled the papers from Paris to Moscow and beyond. The Eastern Bloc, like Brecht, imagined Kraus had abandoned the working class itself when push came to shove. The French grasped that Kraus had been forced to play a hopeless hand against the Nazis. Some Nazis accused Goethe's greatest admirer of "hating Germany,"[37] not to mention the incomparable sin of pacifism, but a Hamburg obituary praised "the authentic pathos of his moralism" as the true spirit of the Old Testament, calling him above all else a rabbi, "perhaps the only *character* in the corrupt world of the Viennese Jews."[38] Kraus had confessed in 1934 that he loved an "uncompromisable" Jewish spirit above all, and one Jewish journal chided those Kraus-haters who loved to parade as assimilated Germans except when it was expedient to hide from the righteous wrath of the "prodigal son."[39] A Catholic journal in Germany urged Christians "to recognize, with astonishment and perhaps with shame, the position this man's pure incorruptibility achieved, at the extreme limit of this mortal world."[40] In 1937, when Kraus's friends installed his monument in Vienna's Central Cemetery, his lawyer said God had recalled his favorite early so he would not have to witness what was about to happen.

In 1938 the Social Democratic candidate Karl Renner, who was to become chancellor and president of the Second Austrian Republic after the war, urged his constituents to support the Nazi annexation of Austria and "our leader Adolf Hitler."[41]

Brecht was so wrong: when the age died by its own hand, Kraus was the other hand. Kraus did exemplify a sort of financial suicide: his charitable donations had exceeded all the interest ever compounded on his trust, and the *Fackel* had swallowed the capital. Its debts were so great that Kann, Heinrich Fischer, and Jahoda and Siegel declined their monetary bequests. *Fackel*s had already been remaindered at 50 percent off if one bought a hundred or more. But it was not Kraus who broke into Kraus's flat in 1938, pried open the glass display to shove a rifle butt through the death mask of Kraus's friend, and disappeared with his remaining papers, including the Shakespeare manuscripts; it was the SS. Kann had rescued what else she could from the *Fackel* offices as she fled to Zurich. The family factories were "aryanized" in a forced sale in 1941; Messerschmidt used one for aircraft parts late in the war. Philip Berger, whom Kraus had selected as editor for the posthumous *Die Sprache* (Language), was disappeared by the Gestapo, as was Lanyi and Kraus's favorite niece.

One day in 1943 an SS officer showed up at Dachau with some volumes "donated" by private Jewish collectors in Vienna. Would prisoners kindly sort them; he was going into the book business. And so it was that from bunk to bunk, not a hundred yards from the long ditch and the odd little dressing room where graffiti seems carved with fingernails, there quietly passed a copy of Karl Kraus's *Letzten Tage der Menschheit:* the very last word in cold comfort.

The "liberalism" Kraus combated now goes by the name of "classical liberalism" or "neoliberalism": homo economicus's cheery technocratic mystery cult of rational self-interest, making many rich yet concealing sadism by the magic sleight of the invisible hand. It was widely dismissed even then as a political antique, a quaint precursor of twentieth-century indeterminism. Yet it remained the dominant "moderate" ideology of the world's dominant power, the United States, where the word *liberal* came to denote social democracy. The conservative American president most qualified to judge was to echo Kraus's position on the nihilistic commercialism and pseudopatriotism of military-industrial-media complexes; and not long thereafter, amid social conventions even more freewheeling than Weimar, the concentration-camp ideology Hitler adapted from Cecil Rhodes would cross-fertilize with ghosts of New World slavery, under the flag of "transcending the welfare state" and "controlling drugs." Amid unprecedented export growth in large-scale armaments, even the nominally more democratic and more Jewish party would endorse the moral beauty of vice prosecutions, domestic military operations, standing police armies, prison labor (paper bags?), prison rape said to involve a new virus Mengele would have enjoyed. Privacy invasion would achieve automation and unaccountability on a world scale the Gestapo and NKVD could envy. Kraus would still have been fighting mad.

■

The publishing history of the aphorisms began when Kraus returned from Norway after Annie Kalmar's death in 1901 to find his printer had stolen the *Fackel* trademark and copyrighted it under his own name for a "New Fackel." Before justice was done, Kraus had sued him fifteen times, and *Fackel*'s printing had landed permanently in the loyal hands of Georg Jehoda at Jehoda and Siegel.

It was Kraus's high-strung friend Peter Altenberg who first added a few aphorisms to a 1903 *Fackel* essay. This was followed in 1905 by Wilde aphorisms in translation. Finally in March 1906 came the first Kraus epigrams and aphorisms. At first they were "Throwaway Lines," "Sweepings" literally "From the Wastebasket": bits and pieces of essay drafts, like Chamfort's jottings. They were "Prejudices," "Illusions," "Personal," becoming the "Diary." There were also "Phrases" extracted from the Marquis de Sade and "Splinters" by the pseudonymous Kyon.

In 1908 Kraus began collaborating with *Simplicissimus* in Munich; by that autumn, when he founded the German branch of Fackel Publishing in Munich, he had resolved to release his collected aphorisms by Christmas as *Gedanken* (Thoughts), volume 4 of his *Ausgewähite Schriften* (Selected works). Instead they appeared in March 1909 as volume 2, *Sprüche und Widersprüche* (Dicta and contradicta). Volume 1 had been produced by Rosner in Vienna, but for *Sprüche und Widersprüche* Kraus sent the contract on the last day of 1908 to Albert Langen in Munich, producers of *Simplicissimus* and *März* ([The month of] March). The jacket and cover design for the edition of two thousand—two runs of one thousand in succession—were by Kraus's friend Adolf Loos, though a few of the samples created for the bookbinding price quotes also ended up for sale, with Julius Gipkens's period floral cover art.

His first public reading from the aphorisms was not in Austria but in Berlin in January 1910, part of the campaign to promote the direction and goal of the German *Fackel*. After ten years of silent treatment from the press at home, Kraus was grateful for an unusually receptive German audience and a glowing review of *Sprüche und Widersprüche* in *März* by its editor, Hermann Hesse, who said it had "the earnestness of the fool who calls gold gold and filth filth and does not believe the journalist who says filth is gold."[42] He confessed he had been toying with the idea of moving to Germany, but the cost of establishing the *Fackel* there proved too high. Before long, aphorism readings were in demand at home too, so much so that by the end he resented audience disinterest in the past masters at his readings.

Franz Werfel, a *Fackel* contributor, had worked as a reviewer for the debonair Munich publisher Kurt Wolff, who had taken over Rowohlt. At Werfel's urging, Wolff came to Vienna in 1912, the year after Kraus gave up his collaboration with *Sturm*, and succeeded in signing Kraus for a book, although the book never appeared and Kraus annulled the contract a year later. It was Langen who released the 1914 edition of *Sprüche und Widersprüche*. The following year Kraus accepted Wolff's proposal of a "Press for the Writings of Karl Kraus (Kurt Wolff)," which released another edition. For several years Wolff retained Kraus's erstwhile secretary to work on a documentary biography. Then Werfel's satiric trilogy attacking Kraus was performed at the Burg. After trying to dissuade Werfel, Wolff published it in 1921. Kraus broke with Wolff, and though the "Press for the Writings" was not dissolved for several years, that May the Fackel Press of Vienna and Leipzig was born at Jahoda and Siegel. It printed *Sprüche und Widersprüche* in late 1923 for release in 1924, with a new dedication, and though by 1920 Kraus had essentially abandoned the aphorism in favor of the epigram, the book remained in print for the rest of his life.

Nuts and Bolts: *Dicta and Contradicta* from the Translator's Angle

Speaking words means dropping pebbles into a pool, making ripples. The pool is a neural lattice, and the ripples are neural echoes, multidimensional graphs of associations, rhymes, idioms. The translator's job is to find triggers for very similar echoes through a very different lattice.

Kraus's wordplay, neologisms, and sentence structure fanaticism make the risk of dissimilarity that much greater, by crossing the border into prose poetry. Later he would call poetry untranslatable: "You can translate a lead article but not a poem: you can cross the border naked, but not without your skin—unlike clothing, it will not grow back."[43]

This is contradictory coming from a man who thrilled audiences with translations; but here the contradiction is superficial, a calculated half-truth, Kraus's impulse to control every carving stroke on the opponent who is to receive his arrow. Kraus was far from averse to being translated, so long as it was not into Hungarian or Yiddish. He approved an English verse translation by Alfred Bloch, an American painter who had spent youthful German days among the Blaue Reiter. Kraus advertised the translation in a 1930 *Fackel* and entrusted Bloch with one of the two galleys of the *Die dritte Walpurgisnacht*. He was proud of his Sorbonne lectures and annoyed that the Austrian papers ignored them. When he attacked translators who wanted to outdo August Wilhelm Schlegel's Shakespeare, he was glorifying Schlegel too, and he emulated him and Tieck when he himself dared to "translate" *Timon* and even the sonnets. Setting hand to the sonnets is no joke, particularly if you do not read English (prompting Kraus to confess that really he had gone straight to the original Yiddish).

In aiming to turn the common whore of modern language back into a virgin, prevent it from becoming a Trojan horse or mock mirror, Kraus anticipated the later Viennese expatriate philosophy of language games. Linguistic form was not the clothing of a thought but its substance. As Nietzsche had put it, "We cease to think when we refuse to do so under the constraint of language."[44] The sibyl of language took possession of the artist as vehicle for revealing the deeper rules of her game, but as her pronouncements collided with the nonsense of the times they might become paradox to philistine eyes. The artist might have to go outside the world to find the level where the surface contradictions resolve themselves. His mistress's dicta were *Sprüche und Widersprüche,* literally "Sayings and Contradictions."

To preserve the rhyme of *Sprüche und Widersprüche,* English would have to use "Sayings and Naysayings" or "Sayings and Gainsayings"; but these have misleading archaic overtones. So where do we find a common, current, prosaic word like *contradiction* to convey paradox? We go outside the world, we resort to paradox, to a word neither common, nor current, nor prosaic, nor even existent: *Contradicta. Dicta and Contradicta.*

Though he warned of their abuse as a symptom of linguistic cancer, such neologisms are a Kraus hallmark.[45] By compressing multiple associations to critical mass, they explode humorously with the neglected philosophical gifts implicit in language. Like his German predecessor Georg Friedrich Christoph Lichtenberg, Kraus was fond of analogies from elementary maths, and you might say he traveled from hackneyed phrases and provincialism to abstraction via wordplay in much the same way mathematicians travel from tedious axioms to surprising theorems via substitutions. Where the mathematician startles by busting open a simple algebraic expression into an infinite trigonometric series, the aphorist can startle by busting open a cliché through the long series of unfamiliar associations from a cognate concept or similar-sounding word. In both cases the new formulas may have a surprisingly large range of application, even where the substitute series do not, as the mathematicians say, converge. They are half-truths yet one-and-a-half: imaginary numbers to trace complex roots of social decay.

Instead of exacerbating Kraus's "untranslatability," this often works equally well in English, offering new and fair ways of escorting him across the border. Take his claim that culture has made women into *Galanteriewaren* (lingerie, goods for gallantry), that its spiritual influence has degenerated into plastic surgery on *femina economica*. You could preserve the exchange aspect of this with the flat "luxury goods," but the imaginary "camisouls" implicitly does the same without diluting the erotic context. The *Zitatenprotz,* the snobby showoff who mangles ancient quotes, can resolve to a "quotial climber." When Kraus smells a rat in the literature factory and asks how he manages so much *nicht lesen* (not reading), English answers with an imaginary split infinitive: "time to not read." With one imaginary letter it conveys the transparency of his *Unterleibeigenschaft,* merging *Unterleib* (nether parts) with *Leibeigenschaft* (serfdom, chattel slavery): "privates ownership." When he creates *Fischweiblichkeit* to graft the shrill *Fischweib* (fishwife) onto *Weiblichkeit* (femaleness, femininity), English tempts us with the literal "fishwifeliness," but even today "wifeliness" retains marital Griselda overtones missing in "femaleness" and in the imaginary solution "feminagity."

More often English already offers analogues to German associations or word pairs that merge naturally. For *Bullen* (bulls, big shots) we have "dominant apes"; for *Instrumenten,* the naturalized "apparatchiks." By playing on *genus* (species) and *genuss* (enjoyment), German linguistic history gets down to the brass tacks of birth, copulation, and death; Kraus could have come very close to this in English by observing that his higher-octane girlfriends found the distinction between organismic vitality and orgasm little more than a question of spelling. When he says he was seldom *verliebt* (in love, processed by love), always *verhasst* (hated, processed by hate), English offers "beguiled" and "reviled." For old tomes that can be *unverständlich* (incomprehensible) or *selbstverständlich* (self-evident) we have "arcane" and "mundane." The time that *vergeht* (passes on) for the philistine and *besteht* (stands firm) for the artist can "pass" or "mass." The *Hausherrlichkeit* of the star actor at center stage, mixing *Hausherr* (lord of the manor) and *Herrlich* (superb, masterful), flows naturally into "magnificentrality." *Freudenhausbackenheit,* grafting *Freudenhaus* (brothel) onto *hausbacken* (homely, homemade), readily resurfaces as "whorehousewifely."

Some Krausisms can even be transcribed directly into English, such as "controlsexual" for the moral witch-hunt, "emeretrix" for the prostitute emerita, and "cryptogamy" for the velvet coffin of moribund marriage; and some constructions offer the same pun, as with *an-haben* (to have on): X has on clothes, Y has the goods on X.

The hegemony of American "expat" English is a net benefit to Kraus. When he says an aphorism should outwing the truth, get beyond it with a *Satz,* he is recommending both a "leap" and a "sentence." The new lingua franca offers "spin," a low-overhead, four-letter word combining the ideas "concise phrase" and "agile motion." The test pilot's "envelope," the trader's "coupon," the "meat market," the "airhead," the "player," the "sales rep," and the earthy dialect of the American South analogous to Austrian German have now been bounced to viewers all over the English-Speaking Union and beyond for decades. Kraus's cause is also furthered by occasional veiled expatriate American allusions: T. S. Eliot's Sweeney seems to have had innumerable relatives in Kraus's Vienna, and at one point Kraus—of all people—withholds his essence from women.

Despite all these techniques, there are wordplay monsters that have to be lamed rather than slain. In German Kraus's pedants confuse the palindromes "life" and "fog"; in English, "live" and "evil." "Evil" may introduce disorder, but it is an abstraction and not always a moral fog. When Kraus says literally "dignity [*Würde*] is the conditional form of what one is," *Würde* also means the conditional "would." Equating "dignity" and "would" seems to have neither real nor complex roots in English, but rendering "dignity as the conditional form of the human verb" puts us well over the top. Kraus says the *Grenze,* or border, most tempting to smugglers is the *Altersgrenze,* the age of consent, the "age border": the pederast presses beyond diminishing returns the observation that the shorter the visible line of ghosts at the bedside, the less blatant the resemblance between the lover and the trick. Here "limit" and "age limit" would be wooden, "boundary" even more so. But "border" by itself has already implicitly revealed what German has to say here about emotional territory.

Multiple translations can serve as a broad-spectrum antibiotic against misunderstanding. When Kraus says "the bigger the boot, the bigger the heel," the literal English captures the subtext pun on worldly power and moral depravity but misses the primary overtone of mass-market fraud rather than force and the secondary overtone of a writing passage. We can approach the range of associations using a kaleidoscope of variants as a run-up to the literal rendering. Likewise with Kraus's play on the *Stimmung,* or mood, of the Viennese being like the tuning of an orchestra. The association between a good-tempered person and a well-tempered clavier is nowhere near as explicit in English but can be amplified using the expression "tuning in," which suggests an initial melee of broadcast frequencies similar to the melee of instruments tuning for a symphony.

Though Kraus sometimes goes out of his way to give fair warning of an allusion, placing explicit bets on the immortality of Lichtenberg and Schopenhauer among others, he despised other people's pedantry and condemned any education that left you able to cite chapter and verse. Also some of his thrusts at contemporary Viennese personalities seem almost certainly calculated to improve with age as time withered the victims' ephemeral celebrity. Still, as with any translation, readability sometimes demands a brief implicit footnote. Even Austrian readers who have never heard of Musaeus or Jean Paul are sure to know the German self-image as the people of *Dichter und Denker,* the nation of poets and philosophers; to them it is obvious what Kraus is up to in calling the Germans *Richter und Henker,* judges and hangmen. But if you let an English reader in on the game only after the fact, the wit loses its fizz.

The translator has to accommodate unusual contradiction in Kraus's view of his language. When asked in wartime how he could sympathize with the English even though he did not even speak English, he said it was because he knew German. The German language was the deepest, German speech the shallowest; linguistic smog in the Germanic countries forced him to recuperate abroad. Schoolboy Latin might teach a boy to be a good writer (though absurdly he must have thought it lost on the French, whose language one used to say such things as "La bourse est la vie"); but school German could guide a boy only into military life. Although he translated and adapted foreign languages and saw himself playing for long-term literary stakes far beyond his contemporary Viennese role, his art is consciously German, and he knew that very occasionally his demand that you read his things twice becomes serious enough to risk "jackass" charges of turgidity. When it comes to hanging and intertwined clauses, High German remains more liberal than High English, where you nearly always put your lucidity cards on the table, just as you take your shoes off in a mosque; and even with Kraus the translator must split or reorder a long period now and then to keep the focus on the author rather than German generally.

Kraus was not bloody-minded about "meteruation" in the epigrams for *Sprüche und Widersprüche,* but they still demand more liberties than the translator could be forgiven elsewhere. So that a woman can be either "fallen" or capable of making philistines "fall" for her, she becomes either a "fallen queen" or "squeaky-clean," not just morally spotless. "Contempt for prostitution?" becomes "Hookers fill you with contempt?" Libido "triumphs yet again" rather than just "remaining the victor." The composite image of Venus was originally meant only to "live throughout my lifetime." Instead, while he lives "death cannot hope to scar it." This is purple, but so in a way was Kraus's bottom line of devotion, not just to the memory of love but to the contradictory extremes of authenticity and beauty that justify his English passport.

Notes

Unless otherwise noted in the text, the quotations are from Karl Kraus.

1   Quoted in Wilma Abeles Iggers, *Karl Kraus: A Viennese Critic of the Twentieth Century* (Hague: Martinus Nijhoff, 1967), 30.

2   Quoted in Paul Schick, *Karl Kraus in Selbstzeugnissen und Bilddokumenten* (Hamburg: Rowohlt, 1965), 28.

3   Ibid., 123.

4   Ibid., 65.

5   Karl Kraus, *Pro domo et mundo,* in *Karl Kraus: Beim Wort Genommen,* ed. Henrich Fischer (Munich: Kösel, 1965), 335.

6   Arthur Schnitzler quoted in Friedrich Pfäfflin and Eva Dambacher, with Volker Kahmen, *Karl Kraus: Eine Ausstellung des Deutschen Literaturarchivs im Schiller-Nationalmuseum Marbach* (Marbach am Neckar: Deutsche Schillergesellschaft, 1999), 129.

7   Karl Kraus, *Dicta and Contradicta,* item 909 herein.

8   Quoted in Iggers, *Karl Kraus,* 43.

9   Fritz Wittels, *Ezechiel der Zugereiste* (Berlin: Egon Fleischel, 1910).

10 Quoted in Schick, *Karl Kraus,* 107.

11 Pfäfflin and Dambacher, *Karl Kraus,* 197.

12 Quoted in ibid., 111.

13 Ibid., 370.

14 Ibid., 9.

15 Karl Kraus, *Die Fackel,* no. 404 (December 5, 1914): 2.

16 Quoted in Schick, *Karl Kraus,* 90.

17 Ibid., 84.

18 Ibid., 91.

19 Ibid., 68.

20 Adolf Hitler, *Mein Kampf* (Munich: Franz Eher Nachfolger, 1933), 624.

21 Pfäfflin and Dambacher, *Karl Kraus,* 74.

22 Karl Kraus, *Die dritte Walpurgisnacht,* vol. 1 of *Werke,* ed. Henrich Fischer (Munich: Kösel, 1965), 9. See also Jochen Stremmel,

"*Dritte Walpurgisnacht*": *Über einen Text von Karl Kraus* (Bonn: Bouvier Verlag Herbert Grundmann, 1982), 220.

23 Karl Kraus, *Traumstück* (Vienna: Fackel, 1921).

24 Quoted in Pfäfflin and Dambacher, *Karl Kraus,* 281.

25 Quoted in Michael Horowitz, *Karl Kraus* (Vienna: Orac, 1986), 64.

26 Ibid., 86–87.

27 Quoted in Pfäfflin and Dambacher, *Karl Kraus,* 510.

28 Quoted in Schick, *Karl Kraus,* 131.

29 Ibid., 134.

30 Ibid., 133.

31 Quoted in Iggers, *Karl Kraus,* 151.

32 Quoted in Schick, *Karl Kraus,* 110.

33 Quoted in Pfäfflin and Dambacher, *Karl Kraus,* 480.

34 Ibid., 482.

35 Quoted in Schick, *Karl Kraus,* 136.

36 Quoted in Pfäfflin and Dambacher, *Karl Kraus,* 512.

37 Quoted in Richard Lanyi, *Karl Kraus und seine Nachwelt: Ein Buch des Gedenkens,* ed. Michael Horowitz (Vienna and Munich: Christian Brandstätter, 1986), 55.

38 Ibid., 76.

39 Ibid., 73.

40 Ibid., 36.

41 Quoted in Horowitz, *Karl Kraus,* 169.

42 Quoted in Pfäfflin and Dambacher, *Karl Kraus,* 163.

43 Kraus, *Pro domo et mundo,* 245.

44 Friedrich Nietzsche, *Nachlass aus den achtziger Jahren,* vol. 6 of *Werke,* ed. Karl Schlechta (Munich: Carl Hanser, 1980), 862.

45 Breon Mitchell notes a curious dearth of information on Kraus's relation to the author of *Finnegans Wake:* "Is it possible that Joyce, who lived in Trieste for many years when it was still part of the Austro-Hungarian Empire, never even heard of Vienna's most prominent literary satirist?" Breon Mitchell, "Joyce and Kraus: A Theatre on Mars," in *Literary Theory and Criticism: Festschrift in Honor of Rene Wellek,* ed. Joseph P. Strelka (New York: Peter Lang, 1984), 1001.

Notes

Numbers refer to aphorism numbers, not page numbers.

9   A hysteron-proteron—taken from the Greek, meaning "the latter
     (as) the former"—is a figure of speech or an order of nature in
     which what should be last or inferior actually turns out to be first
     or superior. The Bible says that in the beginning was the Word;
     Kraus says the divine Word might have an ironic rhetorical flourish.

36   In William Shakespeare's tragedy *Hamlet* (1604), Prince Hamlet is
     maddened to learn his mother is guilty of adultery with his father's
     murderer.

37   In Shakespeare's comedy *A Midsummer Night's Dream* (1600),
     Oberon, king of the fairies, is jealous of his wife Titania's fondness
     for her page. To divert her affections and have some fun, he squirts
     Cupid's love juice into her eyes to make her infatuated with the
     first creature she sees. This turns out to be an ass, figuratively and
     literally: a ludicrous amateur actor on whom Oberon's goblin and
     jester Puck has placed a donkey's head.

56   Wilhelm Richard Wagner (1813–83) was the symbolist musical and
     political genius of Germanic racial legend and the musical drama.
     Outside the aesthetic realm, Wagner and his wife, Cosima, do not

seem to have needed much instruction from Kraus on the fallacy of sublimation: she was still married to someone else when their first children were born.

62   Procrustes (Damastes) laid visitors on his bed. If they were too short, he racked them up to size; if too long, he trimmed them by amputation.

83   Kraus quotes from Shakespeare's tragedy *King Lear* (1608). Edgar, undone by the treason of his bastard brother, reflects on the advantages of having nothing left to lose.

86   Eros was not necessarily a god, a child, Aphrodite's son, or heterosexual.

87   Socrates of Athens (b. 409 B.C.) was the epitome of the disinterested philosopher-citizen, master of Plato and Xenophon. He resisted the famous charms of the youth Alcibiades, but his virtue did not protect him from capital punishment for corrupting youth. Jack the Ripper was a medically trained serial murderer who dissected prostitutes in Whitechapel, London, in 1888. He taunted the police and was never caught.

90   Xanthippe was the shrewish wife of Socrates of Athens.

102 In *Venus im Pelz* (Venus in furs [1870]), the Austrian novelist Leopold von Sacher-Masoch (1835–95) portrays Severin, whose ultimate payoff is cruel infidelity.

122 Cronus unseated and castrated his father, Uranus, and threw his parts into the sea, forming white foam out of which Aphrodite was born. When Hermes found Zeus on the banks of the Triton with a splitting headache, he summoned the smith god, Haephestus, who cracked open Zeus's head; out sprang Athena, fully armed. Lucina clasped her hands and crossed her legs when Alcemena was in labor with Hercules. These magic postures delayed the birth for a week, so in Rome they were taboo on certain solemn occasions. The "cultured beauty" might muddle myths, but her reproductive instinct is crystal clear.

168 Danaeus ordered his fifty daughters to kill their husbands; most did and were condemned to pour water forever into leaky vessels.

203 In *Faust I* (1798–1808), the German classical literary masterpiece by the national poet Johann Wolfgang von Goethe (1749–1832), the disillusioned scholar Faust sells his soul to the devil for exotica, including intense love for the innocent Gretchen, whom he seduces and abandons to abortion and suicide.

229 The first thing Cicero said when he confronted the seditious Catiline and his allies in the Senate was, "How long? How far will you
abuse our patience, Catiline?" Everyone knew about their arson
and murder plans and wished them dead. Kraus would have seen
this phrase not only at school but also repeatedly at his printers'; it
had been the standard font illustration for centuries. The substitu-
tion of Cato also implies nationalism, ultraconservatism, censorship, and litigiousness.

261 Laws encouraging "privates ownership" (*Unterleibeigenschaft,* a
Krausism) are the opposite of laws against marital rape.

262 Kraus's absent-minded Latin means "prostitution as a paradoxical
route to authenticity."

273 Otto Weininger's *Geschlecht und Charakter* (Sex and character
[1903]) was an apex of both misogyny and Jewish self-hatred, in
some ways a photographic negative of Kraus's sardonic bets on raw
female sexuality. Feminine identity was a horrifying moral void, and
the Jewish male too was in constant danger of melting down into
satanically meaningless sexuality. It was all too much for Weininger;
converting to Protestantism was no help; and in 1903, at the age of
only twenty-three, he shot himself in a rented room.

275 Mnesarete, a Greek hetaera of the fourth century B.C., was nick-
named Phryne, "toad," because of her sallow complexion, but her
charms made her so rich that she offered to rebuild the walls of
Thebes so long as they were inscribed "destroyed by Alexander,
restored by Phryne the courtesan." Dionysus's train included the
maenads, women in a bacchic ecstasy.

281 The saying "Omne animal post coitum triste" means that every
living creature is sad after coitus. It is much older than Christianity
and may go back further than Galen or Aristotle, to whom it is
commonly attributed. It appears in various versions, typically sin-
gling out the human female as an exception. Kraus emphasizes that
post (after) is not necessarily the same as *propter* (on account of).

286 In one version, King Tantalus served his son to the gods when he
invited them to dinner; he was condemned to stand in Tartarus
with abundant water just below and fruit just above, both forever
out of reach.

288 *Don Quixote* (1604) by Cervantes (Miguel de Cervantes Saavedra)
(1547–1615) is an epic parody of traditional Spanish ballads and chiv-

alric romances, where the squire Sancho Panza plays commonsense foil to his crazy dreamer of a master, the erring knight Don Quixote.

291 Kraus ponders the Greek roots of "catholicism," *kata* and *holos:* "concerning [the] whole."

296 The Prater is the Vienna amusement park, with everything from rides to string quartets.

299 Friedrich Nietzsche (1844–1900), the German whom Kraus was to eulogize as the sharpest philosophical mind of his century (after biting his head off for various literary sins), dreamed of a coming master race, the *Uebermensch,* or Hyperhuman, commonly translated "Superman."

328 Mozart's Don Giovanni tries to ravish a lady and kills her outraged father in a duel. Later he comes across a statue of the father, inscribed with a desire for revenge, and issues it a dinner invitation. It actually comes to life, shows up for dinner, drains the life out of Don Juan, and sends him to hell.

383 The loom is where the Spirit fashions the living garment of divinity in *Faust I.*

392 Bismarck is Prince Otto Eduard Leopold von Bismarck-Schönhausen (1815–98), the "iron chancellor" of the German Empire, militarist, royalist, and absolutist, who completely reorganized Germany under Prussian leadership.

394 Some opera lovers scorned Kraus for loving the work of the prolific German Jacques (Jacob) Offenbach (1819–80), the father of French comic operetta and one of the most significant popular composers of the nineteenth century. Kraus's operetta references include Offenbach's *Bataclan* (1855), *Bluebeard* (1866), and *La princesse de Trebizonde* (1869).

396 Kraus refers again to Shakespeare's *Hamlet.*

405 and 410 In his masterpiece, the *Kritik der reinen Vernunft* (Critique of pure reason [1781]), Germany's greatest philosopher, Immanuel Kant (1724–1804), laid the critical foundations of German Idealism, demonstrating the impossibility of knowledge outside certain categorical limits that excluded much traditional theology. Kraus derides the narcissistic feuilleton mentality that truncates the organs of knowledge even further.

425 St. Vitus' dance is Sydenham's (or Rheumatic) Chorea, a brain disorder causing spasms and grimacing. The Echternach monastery was founded by the Anglo-Saxon St. Willibrord (658–739).

427   Edmund is the villainous bastard son of the Earl of Gloucester in Shakespeare's *King Lear.*

428   After an initial rapprochement with Sigmund Freud, Kraus became one of the bitterest contemporary critics of psychoanalysis, and the psychoanalysts in turn ridiculed Kraus and his followers as arrested-development sadists.

451   Kraus is referring to Goethe's *Götz von Berlichingen mit der eisernen Hand* (Götz von Berlichingen with the iron hand [1773]) and to *Die Räuber* (The robbers [1780]) by Friedrich von Schiller (1759–1805), Goethe's companion at the peak of classical German literature. In *The Robbers* Franz von Moor viciously slanders his brother, Karl, until their father disowns Karl. Franz sends Karl a letter about his fate so unctuous that a disgusted reader can only say, So this lowlife is called Franz? Götz is more general but less abstract: "Tell this captain: as always I have all due respect for His Imperial Majesty. But as for him, tell him he can kiss my ———."

455   Kraus is referring to Heinrich (Harry) Heine (1797–1856), the German poet, journalist, and satirist. Although he attacked him many times, Kraus had some common background with Heine. Both were from business families, but Heine went bankrupt as an entrepreneur before going off to university.

456   Siegfried is the noble Teutonic orphan who becomes a great hero in Old Norse and Old German literature.

462   Messina in Sicily was leveled in an earthquake in 1783 and again in 1908.

473   When the youth Narcissus rejected the nymph Echo, Aphrodite punished him by making him pine away for love of his own image, reflected in a fountain as presaging death.

506   Kraus is referring to the German composer Ludwig van Beethoven (1770–1827), who lived in Vienna starting in 1792.

511   Helen was the supremely beautiful daughter of Zeus and Leda, the cause of the Trojan War immortalized in Homer's epic poems.

517   Falstaff is the fat, lovable comic rogue who appears in Shakespeare's history play *Henry IV* (1598) and (distinctly altered) in his comedy *The Merry Wives of Windsor* (1602).

522   Kraus is referring to the German dramatists Ernst von Wildenbruch (1845–1909) and Moritz August von Thuemmel (1738–1817). Sophocles (495–406 B.C.) was one of the three great ancient Greek tragedians.

544 In the *Erdgeist* (Earth Spirit [1895]) and *Büchse der Pandora* (Pandora's box [1903]) by Frank Wedekind (1894–1918), Lulu personifies the criminally pure sexuality that destroys until it meets its match in the purely criminal sexuality of Jack the Ripper.

548 Schiller's most famous dramas are his *Wallenstein* trilogy, first published in 1800.

612 Moltke was a famous German military family that included several chiefs of the general staff.

613 The German poet and playwright Count August von Platen-Hallermünde (1796–1835) mocked Heine in *Der romantische Oedipus* (The romantic Oedipus [1829]). Heine fired back, mocking not only Platen's literary talents but also his sexual preferences.

614 Maximilian Harden (born Maximilian Felix Ernst Witkowski) (1861–1927) was the Berlin publicist and editor of the weekly *Die Zukunft* (The future). He advised Kraus at the founding of the *Fackel,* but Kraus later broke with him over Harden's journalistic failure to respect sexual privacy.

623 In his later years, spinal disease and failing vision kept Heine confined to what he called his "mattress-grave."

629 G. M. Saphir was a mid-nineteenth-century liberal journalist with the Berlin papers *Schnellpost* and *Courier.*

644 Georg Friedrich Christoph Lichtenberg (1742–99) was a German physicist and aphorist heavily influenced by such English and Irish authors as Laurence Sterne, Henry Fielding, and Jonathan Swift.

645 Arthur Schopenhauer (1788–1860) synthesized the insights of Plato and Kant with the Vedanta and Christian mysticism, urging renunciation of this world, where various forms of the same blind will are condemned perpetually to obstruct one another's self-actualization in mutual torment. He was also a grouch with a weakness for women.

648 Jean Paul was the pen name of Johann Paul Richter (1763–1825), a seminal discursive German Romantic author.

651 The most famous German translations of Shakespeare were begun by August Wilhelm Schlegel in 1797–1810 and finished by Ludwig Tieck, his daughter Dorothea, and Count Baudissin in 1825–40.

652 Kraus saw Vienna's Johann Nepomuk Nestroy (1801–62) as the first German-speaking satirist (and actor) in whom language had come to reflect on itself.

657   *Jugend* (Youth [1893]) had been a big hit for the naturalistic German poet and dramatist Max Halbe (1865–1944).

659   Pegasus struck Mount Helicon in Boethia with his foot and out came the Hippocrene, the "fountain of the steed," the fount of the Muses.

701   Heurigen (from *heurige*, new wine) are picturesque taverns in the wine-growing villages outside Vienna, such as Gersthof.

703   Starting in 1896 *Geisha*, somewhat similar to Gilbert and Sullivan's *Mikado*, was a worldwide hit for the London operettist Sidney Jones (1861–1946). There is an apocryphal story that when Galileo found himself forced to abjure the heliocentric theory, he said to himself as he turned to leave the room, "And yet it [the earth] moves." Kraus says that in Italy someone who demanded belief in the constancy of womankind might get similar lip service but not without similar irony.

728   A Panoptikum is a wax museum, though at Kastan's Panoptikum in Berlin there were also live acts, such as tattooed ladies.

732   Lutter and Wegner are still in business in Berlin, still grateful for the custom and mention of the German Romantic author Ernst Theodor Amadeus Hoffman (1776–1822). The German word for sparkling wine is *Sekt* because Hoffman's friend the German Shakespearean actor Ludwig Devrient jokingly shouted for Sack at Lutter's but the waiter, misunderstanding, brought him his usual bubbly.

749   Genghis (d. 1227) was khan, or chief, of the Mongols conquering as far as Iran. Nero Claudius Caesar (37–68) ruled Rome from 54 to 68; his notorious wickedness included murdering his mother and wife and persecuting Christians.

755   The Viennese writer Peter Altenberg (born Richard Engländer [1859–1919]) was Kraus's close friend beginning in 1894.

757   The American Transcendentalist philosopher Ralph Waldo Emerson (1803–82) had a brother, William, who studied theology in Germany in the era of philosophical idealism and demythologizing biblical criticism. Emerson's friends included the philosophical Germanophile Samuel Coleridge but also Thomas Carlyle, the archsatirist of German metaphysical blather.

758   In 1890 the Irish writer Oscar Fingall O'Flahertie Wills Wilde (1856–1900) published the novel *The Picture of Dorian Gray*, a modern aesthetic myth of an ageless English Adonis whose descent into vice

and crime was visible only in the magical world of art. Kraus's admiration for Wilde's masterpiece is palpable throughout *Dicta and Contradicta,* not least in his contempt for fake Dorian Grays.

764   Marcus Junius Brutus (85–42 B.C.) is best known for killing Caesar, but he was also a philosophical writer and orator and a friend of Cicero. Spiegelberg is the cynical libertine who founds the band of robbers in Schiller's *Die Räuber* (The robbers [1780]). He does not end up the leader, but he is a real wit and outlaw, not a dreamer.

783   Achilles is the mythical ancient Greek hero whose mother dipped him in the River Styx, making him invulnerable except at the heel she held while dipping him.

792   As revenge for Prometheus's theft of fire from the gods, Zeus ordered that the woman Pandora be made of earth, beautiful in form but loathsome in cunning. Hermes gave her a jar, or "box," as a dowry. Her shortsighted husband allowed her to open it and release all the evils of the world, closing it in time only to retain the fraud of Hope—a pinch of snuff.

799   Aesculapius, the Greek god of medicine, learned his craft from various magic animals; he is represented by the serpent of rejuvenation and prophecy.

803   The quotial climber jumbles Horace's Pythagorean injunction not to marvel at anything and Plutarch's version of Solon's law not to speak ill of the dead. The result: "Marvel at nothing about the dead."

806   Friedrich Wilhelm Viktor Albert (1859–1941) was Kaiser Wilhelm, the German emperor and Prussian king from 1888 through World War I. He had fired Bismarck in 1890.

816   Science traditionally demands that suffering be minimized by confining experimental vivisection to a "vile body," the lowest and least sensitive organism possible; here Kraus experiments with his own vile body.

817   Bacchus (Dionysus) was god of fertility, particularly the fertile wine grape. His festivals grew so wild that the Senate banned them in 186 B.C.

823   Kraus is referring to Friedrich von Schiller's *Verschwörung des Fiesko* (Fiesco's conspiracy at Genoa [1784]).

903   Kraus quotes from the *Satyricon,* by Nero's leisurely and licentious favorite Petronius Arbiter, Gaius Petronius (d. 66 A.D.).

906   The Chimborazo is the highest mountain peak in Ecuador.

916   Vanessa Io and Vanessa Cardui are the Peacock and Painted Lady
      butterflies. Vanity of vanities, all is vanity, says Ecclesiastes, but
      some vanities are more sustainable than others.

Epigram Index

art: accessibility, 369, 464, 557, 566, 575–78; action, 823; cleansing, 442, 482, 561, 594; creativity, 2, 67, 471, 473, 522, 537, 540, 550, 613, 619, 661; drawing, 551–54; eroticism, 79, 259, 472, 537, 542; expression, 548; female, 127, 129–30, 292; insipid, 515–16, 659; inspiration, 276, 481, 502–3, 547–48, 600, 649, 864; linguistic, 498, 513, 530, 573–82, 613; magician, 899; market, 494, 513, 567, 631, 636; modern, 514, 519, 536; patronage, 487, 631; and philistinism, 353, 371, 373–74, 472, 474, 486, 502–3, 729, 916; politicized, 394, 566–67, 573–74; public, 487–88, 527, 575–77, 639, 838; and science, 503, 549; torture, 102, 643, 680; and virtuosity, 79, 499, 550, 585. *See also* class; creativity; criticism; imagination; language; literature; music; time
—form and content, 562–63, 566–67, 593, 614, 661; conscience, 587, 670, 678; genres, 514, 557; wit, 529, 578, 581
—practicality, 530, 729, 879; common sense, 419, 430, 636, 887; scam, 361, 392
artist: dejection, 471; journalism, 636, 916; mediocre, 547, 659; mutual comprehension, 480; persona, 353; servant, 522, 585, 683; unconscious, 471; vanity,

473, 500. *See also* actor; musician; writer
attribution, 672. *See also* plagiarism
Austria: authenticity, 728, 732–33; celebrity, 700–701; dialect, 308, 328; literature, 102, 529, 652; manners, 313, 328, 416, 708, 715–16; politics, 335, 408, 686, 687, 689, 707, 802. *See also* Altenberg, Peter; Germany; Nestroy, Johann Nepomuk; Vienna
authenticity, 109, 498, 728, 732–33, 834, 872–73. *See also* character; masquerade ball; personality; truth
author. *See* writer
automobile, 370, 374, 397, 720, 731
aviation, 374, 459–60, 592, 651, 736. *See also* tourism
barbershop, 342–44, 412, 596
barrel organ. *See* music
beauty, 427, 484–85, 549, 716–17. *See also* aesthetics; Dorian Gray; Venus; Vienna; women
Being, 312, 466. *See also* categories; existence; life; metaphysics; nature
Berlin, 693, 719, 727–28, 732, 734–35; motion, 716–18, 720. *See also* Germany; Hamburg; Prussia; Vienna
betrayal, 302, 306, 679, 700, 826, 855. *See also* discretion; fidelity; secrecy; sexes
bisexuality, 86–77. *See also* perversity

Bohème, 741, 756

book, 522, 589, 646, 668, 733, 898; females, 2, 126; profession, 602, 604, 647–48. *See also* literature

business, 46, 121, 333, 335, 416, 455, 493, 693, 773, 888. *See also* advertising; art; economics; globalism; literature; media; producer; prostitution

butterfly, 478, 916

categories, 190, 410, 487, 813. *See also* Being; media; metaphysics; morality; psychiatry; time

Cato, 229

celibacy, 94, 129, 136, 220. *See also* chastity

character, 297, 387, 443, 627, 787, 855; dramatic, 394, 512, 656; female, 165, 194. *See also* personality; sexes; talent

chastity, 42, 189, 429, 837. *See also* celibacy; continence

child, 400, 581, 710, 897, 905, 907, 916; education, 197, 201, 385, 434, 441–43, 906; as metaphor, 44, 114, 289, 568, 674, 680, 782; nursery, 427, 890. *See also* abortion; contraception; family; pederasty; sex

civilization, 183, 278, 323, 461–62, 556, 708, 719, 851. *See also* industrialism; nature

class: common crowd, 352, 372, 430, 557; language, 576, 578, 612; masses, 404, 469, 556, 558, 639; political, 360, 382, 483, 864, 875. *See also* literature; phi-

listinism; politics; public; sexes; society; solitude; stupidity

clothing, 80–82, 105, 353, 402, 452; mental, 355, 371, 448, 562, 576, 680. *See also* cosmetology; mask; masquerade ball; women

coachman, 296, 298, 324. *See also* taxi; Vienna

consciousness. *See* mind

continence, 145, 173, 817. *See also* chastity

contraception, 247–48. *See also* abortion

contradiction, 60, 469, 564–65, 824, 826. *See also* antithesis; aphorism; paradox

conversation, 328, 330, 342, 450, 547, 656, 744, 753. *See also* public; sex; society; women

coquetry, 163, 198, 537, 739. *See also* courtesan

cosmetology, 23, 77–78, 129, 515, 537, 732. *See also* clothing; mask; masquerade ball

courtesan, 58, 85, 274–75. *See also* coquetry; prostitution

cowardice, 777, 811. *See also* hero; sexes

creativity, 475, 561, 643, 662, 733. *See also* art; music; sexes

criticism: appreciations, 273, 487, 489, 538, 645, 857; contemptible, 471, 491, 599, 704, 818, 850; gaia, 460–62; literary, 584, 604, 659, 848; polemical, 128, 336, 349, 673, 765, 834, 849, 877, 892; public, 310, 501, 527, 575, 640–41, 649, 851–52; silent

treatment, 490, 842–43; stupidity, 331; theater, 517, 537, 847.
See also art; book; drama; error;
literature; media; morality; outrage; prejudice; reading; satire;
snob; taste; writer

culture, 328, 379, 381, 417, 448,
531, 558, 609, 721; Germanic,
451–53, 699, 722, 728, 733; media, 402, 610, 916. *See also* art;
education; literature; quote;
stupidity; tourism; women

dance, 106, 298, 515, 555, 700. *See
also* masquerade ball

debauchery, 101. *See also* chastity;
morality; prostitution; sexes

deed. *See* thought

degeneration, 184, 354, 680, 702,
907. *See also* media; modernity;
time

dignity, 42, 103, 132, 308, 381,
728, 746, 776. *See also* honor;
morality; politics

discovery, 380, 556, 665. *See also*
insight; progress; science

discretion, 306, 472, 679, 769. *See
also* betrayal

divinity. *See* religion

Don Juan (character), 42, 328

Don Quixote (character), 288

Dorian Gray (character), 758. *See
also* aesthete; beauty; criticism;
sexes; snob

drama, 204, 442, 454, 522–26,
529–30, 611, 649, 656–57. *See
also* actor; nature; theater

dream, 133, 459, 630, 717, 732,

782, 894–95, 902–3, 908. *See
also* fantasy; imagination; sleep

duplication, 404. *See also* imitation

ecology, 459–62, 916–17. *See also*
civilization; environment; industrialism

economics, 239–43, 264, 362,
456–57, 712, 768, 798–99. *See
also* advertising; business; politics; profit; prostitution; sex

education, 374, 442–50, 510–11,
602, 608, 701, 803, 845. *See also*
child; culture; morality; pedantry; quote; reading; religion; sex

Emerson, Ralph Waldo, 757

environment, 326–27, 369, 442,
721, 751, 898, 912. *See also* ecology; industrialism; public

envy, 239, 300, 786, 835, 863, 875.
See also jealousy; vanity

Eros, 71, 86, 129. *See also* eroticism

eroticism, 83–84, 88, 114, 116,
429; nudity, 79; obstacles, 71,
96–98, 139, 200, 700; rank, 95,
121, 297; thought, 42, 60–61,
68, 174, 181, 259, 274. *See also*
morality; perversity; playboy;
sex; sexes; sexuality; thought

error, 869. *See also* criticism; stupidity

eternity, 297, 367, 572, 696, 738,
891, 913–14. *See also* immortality; religion

evil, 306, 396, 407, 496, 670, 837,
880. *See also* morality; religion;
wickedness

evolution, 374, 378, 419, 642. *See also* adaptation; industrialism; modernity; progress

existence, 13, 345, 461, 751. *See also* Being; life

experience, 44, 61, 443, 853, 860, 905; literature, 256, 492, 685, 833. *See also* wisdom

family, 193, 354–57, 401, 434. *See also* child; marriage

fantasy, 374, 430, 730, 732, 813, 815, 865; erotic, 68, 85; performance, 530. *See also* imagination

fashion, 414, 448, 537, 596, 836. *See also* clothing; form; masquerade ball; style

fata Morgana, 732, 821. *See also* creativity; dream; imagination; psychology

father-confessor, 119, 429. *See also* psychiatry; religion

feeling, 94, 120, 157, 189, 300, 318, 355, 710, 732. *See also* anesthesia; sexes

fetishism, 42, 80–81, 105. *See also* clothing; perversity

feuilleton. *See* media

fidelity, 42–43, 151, 159, 236, 303, 856. *See also* betrayal

food, 323, 340–41, 697–99, 708, 712, 723, 725, 732–33. *See also* nourishment; Vienna

forgiveness, 81, 164, 237, 570, 608, 826, 828–29, 861. *See also* guilt

form, 306, 556, 559, 570, 581, 593, 776. *See also* art; fashion; style

freedom, 381, 680, 741, 844; sexual, 256, 258; social, 385, 388, 687, 732. *See also* politics; prison; sex; sexes

frustration, 30, 132, 145, 185, 294, 632, 643, 909. *See also* morality; prison; repression; stupidity; Tantalus

gallantry, 109, 210, 265, 293. *See also* aesthete; form; society; women

genius, 27, 43, 58, 451. *See also* character; originality; personality; sexes; talent

German language, 56, 205, 308, 337, 442, 567, 577, 782. *See also* Heine, Heinrich

Germany: letters, 102, 204, 617, 629–30, 657–58, 680, 807; philosophy, 452–53, 757, 807; politics, 398, 690, 806–7; society, 277, 314, 434, 451, 706–7, 807. *See also* Austria; Goethe, Johann Wolfgang; Götz von Berlichingen; Gretchen (character); Harden, Maximilian; Heine, Heinrich; Lichtenberg; Prussia; Richter, Johann Paul; Schiller, Friedrich; Schlegel, August Wilhelm; Schopenhauer, Arthur; *Youth* (Halbe)

globalism, 375. *See also* business; ecology; economics; politics

Goethe, Johann Wolfgang, 451, 701–2, 716, 732

Lourdes, 426
love, 239, 363, 472, 487, 568, 669,
    700, 717; Christian, 124–25,
    301, 462; language, 92, 205,
    209, 685, 782; patria, 317–18,
    884. *See also* eroticism; ideal;
    religion; romanticism; science;
    sex; sexes; Venus
—sexual, 55, 59, 92, 196, 205,
    252, 739, 815; mercenary, 239–
    41; wittol, 161–62
madness, 414, 419, 435, 439. *See*
    also psychiatry
marriage, 121, 136, 740–41; adul-
    tery, 47, 117, 151, 163, 207–8,
    212, 284; fraud, 153–54, 274,
    789; monogamy, 233–34, 793–
    95; prostitution, 193, 207. *See*
    also family; sexes
mask, 540
masochism, 102, 104, 680. *See also*
    art; sexes
masquerade ball, 47, 296, 873
masturbation, 138, 140
materialism, 240–41, 461. *See also*
    ecology; prostitution
mathematics, 112, 274, 442, 587,
    634
media: attack, 666–67, 779, 830,
    834, 849; brain rot, 324, 374,
    378, 402–3, 642, 680; culture,
    402, 577, 610; dialect, 654, 840;
    editor, 319, 641, 762, 784; head-
    line, 408, 802; humor, 412–13,
    582, 613, 635; liberal, 407, 420;
    magazine, 413, 595, 608; mere-
    tricious, 406, 636–37; metaphys-
    ics, 409–11, 419–20, 572, 634,

801; military, 415, 561, 593;
    personality, 412, 610, 612, 626;
    pollution, 256, 561, 610, 916;
    publicist, 617; pundit, 577, 610,
    634; Sunday magazine, 498,
    577, 596–97, 632, 654, 729, 916;
    video, 461. *See also* advertising;
    criticism; literature; politics;
    writer
medicine: arts, 475, 516, 531; ex-
    cretion, 786–87; female, 7, 146,
    297; psychosomatic, 330, 426,
    433, 901; ripoff, 454, 798–99.
    See also neuresthenia; optimism;
    psychiatry
memory, 27, 44, 48, 84. *See also*
    sexes
men: dominance, 9, 19–21, 183,
    187, 837; egotism, 4, 22, 134,
    138, 140, 155, 157, 501, 907;
    imagination, 78, 102, 138, 140;
    inner life, 34, 80, 82, 148, 157,
    328, 393; inspiration, 276, 481,
    600, 864; jealousy, 23, 42, 47,
    164, 170, 231, 240, 793; magna-
    nimity, 28, 168–69, 174, 239,
    297, 299, 328, 359, 363, 386,
    539, 768, 868; marriage, 47,
    151, 153–54, 163, 274, 334, 741,
    793; mind, 36, 47, 49, 66, 91,
    174, 181, 275, 363, 504, 600;
    sensuality, 184, 266, 816; vanity,
    169, 712, 716, 726, 739, 764,
    863. *See also* actor; artist; hero;
    military; philistinism; playboy;
    politician; sexes; sport
—love, 19–21, 55, 59, 97, 103,
    164, 239, 240–41, 484, 739;

571, 692. *See also* Cato; decency; eroticism; evil; guilt; law; mistress; outrage; privacy; prostitution; public; scandal; sexes; society; virtue; wickedness

music: conceptual, 759; dissolution, 505; hysteria, 203, 276, 346, 847; inspiration, 276, 548; light, 298, 506, 507–8, 569, 712, 820; modern, 276, 504, 536; nerves, 203, 276, 346, 847; noise, 507–9; opera, 510, 512–14; operetta, 394, 510–14, 634, 703; politicized, 454, 573, 677; public, 575, 716, 751, 772; sexuality, 38, 106, 110, 276; thought, 181, 504

musician, 38, 106, 547, 573, 575, 677, 772, 906

nationalism. *See* politics

nature, 31, 34, 188, 459–62, 658, 905, 916–17; drama, 274, 737. *See also* Being; civilization; environment; industrialism

near-human, 329

neighbor, 301. *See also* Christianity

nerves. *See* anesthesia; hysteria; music; neuresthenia; psychiatry

Nestroy, Johann Nepomuk, 529, 652

neuresthenia, 348. *See also* anesthesia; psychoanalysis

newspaper. *See* media

nourishment, 2, 22, 59, 102, 280, 297, 413, 417, 463, 474, 617, 625, 771

Oberon (character), 37

Offenbach, Jacques, 510–11. *See also* music

opinion, 563–66, 568–69, 577–78, 612, 614, 762, 855. *See also* illusions; intellect; thought; writer

optics, 194, 326, 733, 748

optimism, 814. *See also* hope

Orient, 230, 379, 407, 703

originality, 493, 600–601, 761, 766. *See also* imitation; plagiarism

outrage, 309, 318, 353, 461, 638–39, 641, 713, 746, 831; intellectual, 36, 273, 510, 653, 669, 903. *See also* decency; morality; scandal

Pandora's box, 792

paradox, 832. *See also* antithesis; aphorism; contradiction

pedantry, 437, 680, 813. *See also* culture; education

pederasty, 222–23. *See also* child; sexuality

personality, 374, 469, 655, 870; lack, 517–18, 559, 610, 612, 626, 732, 916; talent, 85, 465, 467, 498, 526; worldview, 468, 566. *See also* actor; character; media; sexes

perversity, 85, 89, 92, 99, 102, 188, 283. *See also* bisexuality; fetishism; homosexuality; incest; masturbation; morality; pederasty; sodomy; voyeurism

pet, 136, 187, 851

philistinism, 191, 353, 413, 484, 498, 797, 870. *See also* art; culture; public philosophy, 652, 757, 759, 891. *See also* media; metaphysics; science; thought

plagiarism, 582, 598. *See also* education; originality; quote

playboy, 67, 69, 87. *See also* courtesan; eroticism; men; prostitution

Poe, Edgar Allan, 643

poet, 41, 891; businessman, 455, 492, 631; other arts, 508, 531; personality, 546–47, 888; well-read, 476, 478–79. *See also* actor; Goethe, Johann Wolfgang; Heine, Heinrich; Nestroy, Johann Nepomuk; Saphir, G. M.; Schiller, Friedrich; Shakespeare, William

poetry, 369, 522–24, 620, 629, 702, 717, 818. *See also* drama; language; literature; poet

police, 226–27, 239, 320–21, 692, 700, 750

politician, 297, 393, 559–60, 837, 880

politics: agitator, 255, 399, 567, 611, 770; brutality, 395, 454, 463, 721, 837, 880, 883–84; bureaucracy, 165, 319, 321, 333, 335, 688, 691, 702, 749, 775; censorship, 804; conservatism, 396, 418, 546, 689, 695, 733, 800, 804, 867; cowardice, 667, 777; democracy, 265, 316, 327, 382, 386, 390, 612, 707, 790; diplomacy, 391, 408, 613, 802; feminism, 58–59, 260–65, 267, 269–71, 388, 790–91, 796; government, 297, 336, 353, 390, 394, 418, 716, 733; humanitarianism, 381, 384, 430, 443, 463; human rights, 385–86, 443, 458, 707, 776; liberalism, 360, 384, 397–98, 407, 420, 440, 612, 707, 808; misanthropy, 316, 463; morality, 255, 837; parties, 612, 778, 837; policy, 374, 376–77, 867; progressive, 385, 417, 442–43; showbiz, 391–94, 483; Tarot, 393; tribalism, 316–18, 334, 689, 884; writing, 319, 546, 609, 666–67, 834. *See also* art; Austria; barbershop; class; dignity; economics; freedom; Germany; globalism; humanity; ideal; law; media; misanthropy; public; society

pornography, 660

power, 297, 388, 454, 768, 883. *See also* politics

prejudice, 316, 398, 811–12, 824, 864. *See also* criticism; psychology

press. *See* media

prison, 366, 643, 687. *See also* freedom; mistress; solitude

privacy, 225, 227, 341, 356, 547, 663, 717. *See also* class; decency; law; mind; morality; public; solitude

Procrustes, 62, 68, 461, 531

producer, 58, 176, 330, 471, 476, 493, 605, 614, 721. *See also* business; creativity; industrialism; originality; sex

profit, 195, 331, 878

Siegfried, 456, 783, 906
silence, 12, 52, 181, 337, 351, 477, 642, 709. *See also* criticism; public
sleep, 221, 335, 459, 467, 630, 717, 900–902, 906; sleepwalker, 178, 546. *See also* dream; mind; stupidity
snob, 487, 489, 758
society, 211, 274, 311–13, 354, 363, 367–68, 418; mindlessness, 322–23, 563, 717; social climbing, 103, 198, 458, 803, 854; social policy, 374, 376–77, 416; vulgarity, 47, 341, 772. *See also* Bohème; class; family; food; gallantry; morality; politics; sexes; snob; solitude; Vienna
sodomy, 217. *See also* perversity
solitude, 364–67, 687, 710, 738, 811, 874; sexual, 94, 140, 235; artistic, 353, 364. *See also* class; society
spiritualism, 414. *See also* metaphysics
spirituality, 309, 461, 484, 496, 559, 693, 699; art, 471, 547; psychiatry, 429, 432. *See also* military; religion; sexes
sport, 177, 274, 401, 559, 892
stage. *See* actor; actress; drama; theater
stupidity, 310, 328, 461, 643, 691, 742, 881, 909; contagion, 330, 441; cultural, 340, 370, 394, 446, 487, 587, 608; political, 316, 385, 394–95, 399, 443, 458, 695, 837. *See also* absurdity; airhead;

error; idiocy; near-human; philistinism; public; sleep
style, 473, 577, 613–14, 617, 671, 680, 770. *See also* clothing; fashion; form; language; literature; writer
sublimation, 125, 131, 274, 537, 542. *See also* creativity; repression; sexes
suffering, 670, 705, 820, 833, 871. *See also* anesthesia; happiness; masochism; medicine; psychiatry; sadism; sexes; stupidity
suicide, 363, 443, 910, 917. *See also* frustration; prison; renunciation
Sunday, 416, 710, 752. *See also* media
Superman, 299. *See also* hero; ideal; politics
superstition, 897. *See also* reason
talent, 85, 465–67, 495–98, 540, 547, 632, 660, 680. *See also* character; creativity; originality; women
Tantalus, 286
taste, 25, 36, 341, 462, 556, 614, 700, 732, 747. *See also* criticism; public
taxi, 331, 671, 713, 730. *See also* coachman
theater, 519, 532–34, 536, 544–45, 703, 741; naturalism, 515, 517–18, 535, 657; performance, 529–31, 538, 654, 656; solitary, 339, 364. *See also* actor; actress; criticism; drama; modernity; music; politics; public

35–36, 47, 121, 136, 151, 163, 193, 197, 207–8, 274, 741; motherhood, 10, 57–59, 179, 193, 206, 290, 581, 701; optics, 149, 181; orthography, 10; sensuality, 1, 6, 12, 28, 44, 49, 79, 85, 183–84, 504, 864; spirituality, 4, 42, 44; talent, 27, 234, 537, 540, 739; vanity, 25, 90, 143, 863, 866. *See also* coquetry; courtesan; love; marriage; menstruation; misogyny; prostitution; sex; sexes

—beauty, 67–74, 84, 129, 141–42, 181, 916; class, 121, 132, 298; elixir vitae, 297, 837; mind, 23, 51–52, 109, 122, 175, 294, 511, 537; romanticism, 121; vice, 195, 239, 272

—exterior, 79, 129–30, 147, 149; artworks, 129–30, 292; clothing, 52, 79–82, 105, 296, 732; cosmetics, 23, 77–78, 537; features, 75–76, 110, 537

—identity, 13–15, 66, 84–85, 97–98, 129, 135, 142, 179, 268, 275; aging, 12, 36, 243, 692; personality, 5, 16–17, 26, 48, 194, 210, 274

—mind, 114, 122, 126, 169, 185, 266, 274–75, 297, 363, 816; consciousness, 55, 152; drives, 101, 108; judgment, 62–64; memory, 27, 44, 48, 122; sterility, 2, 50–53, 66; unconscious, 5, 14–15, 28, 55, 152, 175, 178; wisdom, 54; wit, 52, 275; worldview, 62, 858

—morality, 4, 28–29, 44, 132, 192, 194, 234, 236–38, 244, 272, 388; charity, 124–25, 135; fallen, 26, 190, 192, 197, 205, 207, 246; fidelity, 43, 115, 117–19, 150–51, 158, 163–65, 170, 236; modesty, 42, 52, 79, 87, 93, 129, 262; respectability, 29, 198, 201, 205, 209, 237, 313; shame, 120; virtue, 123, 199

—sexuality, 7, 22, 25, 35–40, 46, 110–15, 121–22, 125; accessibility, 11, 42, 56, 65, 185–86; anesthesia, 36, 113; conquest, 65, 144; frustration, 30; health, 108; inhibition, 35, 273; initiation, 19–20; intimacy, 45; manipulation, 111, 683; mercenary, 107, 121, 167–68, 231–32, 234, 240; objectification, 40; orthography, 10; promiscuity, 25, 32; sadism, 111, 135, 791; satisfaction, 12, 139, 271; sentimentality, 11, 24, 121, 133; sex appeal, 138–42, 173; sublimation, 108, 114, 125, 274, 537, 542

—value, 94, 129, 134–35, 149, 169, 174, 182, 205, 314; sexual, 132, 136–46, 166, 191

work, 103, 186, 379, 382, 417–18, 716, 729, 875; mental, 472, 556, 604, 680

worldview, 62, 440, 468, 589, 733, 761, 813, 858. *See also* thought

writer: afterthoughts, 680–81; bad, 584; development, 588, 602; ephemerality, 572, 596, 836; invective, 574, 733, 781;

language, 442, 562, 574–82, 585, 613–14, 624, 680; originality, 587, 598–601, 780; personality, 626–28, 632–33, 654–55, 677; pornography, 660; public, 561, 577, 608, 631, 640–41, 681, 763, 841; scribbler, 256, 259, 350, 453, 577, 582, 596, 599, 623, 629, 635, 835; style, 586, 589, 612, 608, 613–14, 623–26,

668, 782. *See also* book; criticism; language; literati; literature; media; plagiarism; poet; pornography; women

writing, 604–6, 653, 668, 676, 680, 682, 846; comprehensibility, 565–67, 569, 577, 614, 618; opinion, 562, 563–68, 571, 573–74, 577, 638

Youth (Halbe), 657

Karl Kraus was born in Bohemia in 1874 but spent most of his life in Vienna. In 1899 he founded the journal *Die Fackel* (The torch), which established him as Vienna's most brilliant wit and Europe's leading satirist during the first three decades of the twentieth century. His ferocious opposition to media corruption, stultifying conformity, and militarism climaxed in his major dramatic work, *The Last Days of Mankind*, a notorious attack on war and the cult of high-technology speculation. Of Kraus's many works in poetry, drama, translation, and socioliterary criticism, the most accessible and enduring are the three volumes of aphorisms culled from *Die Fackel*, of which *Dicta and Contradicta* is the first. He died in 1936, not long after finishing *The Third Witches' Sabbath*, the culmination of more than a decade of attacks on Nazism.

Jonathan McVity, born in Boston, Massachusetts, has a degree in English from Oxford University. He was in the art business in Germany and in California before moving to Virginia, where he translated *Dicta and Contradicta* and the maxims and reflections of Vauvenargues as a partner at 20th Century Art and Antiques in Charlottesville and Keene.

Typeset in 10/14 Galliard
with Galliard display
Designed by Erin Kirk New
Composed by Jim Proefrock
at the University of Illinois Press
Manufactured by Thomson-Shore, Inc.

University of Illinois Press
1325 South Oak Street
Champaign, IL 61820-6903
www.press.uillinois.edu